Essentials of
Educational Technology

□ *Essentials of Classroom Teaching Series* □

Essentials of
Educational Technology

James E. Schwartz
Houghton College

Robert J. Beichner
North Carolina State University, Raleigh

Allyn and Bacon

Boston   London   Toronto   Sydney   Tokyo   Singapore

Vice President, Editor in Chief, Education: Sean W. Wakely
Senior Editor: Virginia Lanigan
Editorial Assistant: Bridget Keane
Marketing Managers: Ellen Dolberg and Brad Parkins
Editorial Production Service: Chestnut Hill Enterprises, Inc.
Manufacturing Buyer: Suzanne Lareau
Cover Administrator: Jennifer Hart

Internet: www.abacon.com

Between the time Website information is gathered and published, it is not
unusual for some sites to have closed. Also, the transcription of URLs can result
in typographical errors. The publisher would appreciate notification where these
occur so that they may be corrected. Thank you.

Library of Congress Cataloging-in-Publication Data

Schwartz, James E.
     Essentials of educational technology / James E. Schwartz, Robert
J. Beichner.
         p.   cm.
     Includes bibliographical references and index.
     ISBN 0-205-27700-4 (pbk.)
     1. Education, Elementary—United States—Computer-assisted
instruction.   2. Educational technology—United States.   3. Internet
(Computer network) in education—United States.   I. Beichner,
Robert J.   II. Title.
     LB1028.43.S36   1998
     372'.0285—dc21   98-16159
                                                                        CIP

Printed in the United States of America

10 9 8 7 6 5 4 3   03 02 01 00

Contents

Preface

Just as there was a need for "essentials" textbooks in each of the major elementary school subject areas, there is a need for a concise text that focuses on educational computing, a text that provides a simple theme that illustrates the field of educational computing in light of that theme. This text provides such a theme in what we call the "Delta Principle."

The Delta Principle presents the idea that technology has the capability to *change* the way we think. There are three steps involved in this change process: First, a new technology allows us to do jobs we've always done, but usually faster or with less effort. Second, when we begin to better understand the technology, we discover that it allows us to do new things that we hadn't considered possible before. And finally, we begin to change the way we think about the job we're doing. This third stage represents a stage in which we depend on the technology, and our very notion of what we're doing is shaped by the capabilities of the technology. There are both positive and negative features associated with these changes. The Delta Principle may apply to all types of technology, but this text uses the Delta Principle as a lens through which to view educational uses of computers.

Another unique feature of this text is the attention given to the World Wide Web as an educational resource. Since the web is changing so quickly, we've connected the text to Allyn and Bacon's home page where we periodically update appropriate educational links that are referred to in the text. With the federal government and private industry in general agreement about the urgency of connecting all U.S. schools to the web, there is an urgent need for teacher education to focus on this new resource. Every chapter provides some consideration to the web as an educational resource.

This combination of three design features—the small size of the book (essentials), the Delta Principle as an organizational theme, and the information about the World Wide Web—makes this text a valuable and useful tool for pre-service teacher education courses. It is also useful and helpful in the ongoing effort to provide faculty development for in-service teachers.

We want to acknowledge the contributions of the following reviewers: Lloyd D. Davis, the University of Tennessee at Chattanooga; Cathy Gunn, Northern Arizona University; and Dr. Michael Land, Midwestern State University, Texas.

1 Today's Classroom

LOOKING AHEAD

Do you remember what the last day of school felt like when you could begin your summer vacation? If you grew up in the United States and went to school here, you almost certainly had that experience, and your experience was almost certainly nearly identical to that of your classmates as well as the experience of your parents. Some things in education really don't change very much. That last-day-of-school phenomenon is one of them.

In contrast to that, there are some things in education that are undergoing very deep and fundamental changes today. After decades of mostly unsuccessful efforts to bring about some needed changes in education, we are today seeing changes at a relatively rapid pace. Technology is a major impetus for these changes.

CAN YOU?

- Describe the role(s) educational "standards" are playing in the United States?

- Identify three areas of technology that are important to education at the beginning of the twenty-first century?

- Outline the major events of educational computing since 1980?

- Explain why two major communities of computer-users (Macintosh and PCs) exist?

1

- Describe the current situation in terms of computer use in schools in the USA?

- Differentiate between the ways that technology is used in affluent schools as compared with disadvantaged schools?

TEACHER LABORATORY

Create a thematic teaching unit for grade four. The unit is to center on the Erie Canal. It should incorporate history, geography, mathematics, science, reading, and language arts. Use technology as much as possible.

One teacher approached the preceding task in the following way. He spent an afternoon looking for Internet resources on the Erie Canal. A Yahoo! search turned up thousands of hits on the the search term "Erie Canal." Since this teacher lived near Buffalo, New York, he began his search with sites connected with Buffalo's history.

One of the first interesting facts he found was that on the day of the opening of the Erie Canal cannons were fired to signal the opening. The first cannon was fired at Buffalo, the second was east of Buffalo but within earshot of the first. When the operator of the second cannon heard the opening shot, he fired his cannon. This chain of cannon signals continued along the entire length of the canal, all the way to New York City. The teacher turned this fact into a learning center. He provided a laminated outline map of New York State showing the locations of all the cannons. The information on the Internet supplied the fact that it took 81 minutes for the signal to travel from Buffalo to New York (the fastest communication of an event ever to occur as of 1825!). The teacher provided reference books for children to find the speed of sound. He also provided an atlas so they could find the distance from Buffalo to New York. A series of mathematics and science questions formed the task of this learning center: How long would it have taken the sound to reach New York if one very loud cannon could have been used instead of a chain of cannons? Why did it actually take longer than this? How long did each cannonneer delay (on average) between hearing the preceding shot and firing his cannon?

Another interesting fact gleaned from the Internet was that the canal was forty feet wide and four feet deep. The teacher planned to spend one afternoon marking the height of four feet and the length of forty feet in the hallway outside his classroom. He then used a computer drawing program to prepare a scale drawing of the forty-foot wide channel, and prepared a set of questions asking children to use the same program to draw and measure scale-sized boats that would fit in the canal. He pointed out some reference materials they could use to find out if their calculations were correct.

In his research he began to notice several different years in which the population of Buffalo was reported. He decided to make a spreadsheet activity out of these dates and populations. Children would be asked to make a spreadsheet in which the years from 1800 to 1995, counting by 5's, were listed. In the next column they were to write the population for whatever years they could find. They were to turn their data into a line graph that showed the growth of Buffalo's population over the years. The teacher guessed that the graph would show the dramatic increase in Buffalo's population in the years immediately following the opening of the Erie Canal.

One other resource that the teacher found on the Internet was a number of colorful stories about life in Buffalo in the Erie Canal days. He decided to select a few of these stories that were most appropriate for children and have them read them and then make up a similar fictional multimedia story of their own.

As a culminating project he planned to have children create a multimedia presentation showing what they learned about Buffalo and the Erie Canal in a short HyperStudio stack. He planned to suggest to them that they include their presentation in their electronic portfolios.

How would you approach the task of creating a technology-based thematic teaching unit?

STANDARDS AND REFORM: THE PLACE OF TECHNOLOGY

National Educational Goals and the Meanings of "Standards"

If you had to choose one word to characterize the condition of public education in the United States at the end of the twentieth century, that word would probably be *reform.* For at least the last decade of this century America has been zealously engaged in reform of public education. The term, like so many others that are popular in education today, is conveniently vague. Most participants agree that our agenda is reform; however, there is no universal understanding or agreement about what *reform* means. The elements of reform that do seem to be universal are these: a perception that our public education system is in need of improvement; a belief that higher "standards" are needed along with greater accountability for the use of public money; a conviction that somehow technology should be a major part of this reform. Beyond these general themes there is vast disagreement about the specifics. The general direction of reform is due, in part, to the Goals 2000 legislation, which began with a summit of the nation's governors in 1989. These goal statements were almost impossibly vague and general. What they lacked in specificity, however, they made up for in emotion. They provided a rallying point for much-needed resources to be directed toward the improvement of education.

At the same time the nation was committing itself to becoming "first in the world in math and science achievement," the nation's mathematics teachers were releasing the first of their three "standards" documents (National Council of Teachers of Mathematics, 1989). These mathematics standards described a mathematics curriculum that emphasized problem solving, reasoning, communication, and mathematical connections. During the 1990s these mathematics standards have had far-reaching effects on the mathematics programs in our schools. Educational leaders in other disciplines, observing the effects of the NCTM standards, followed suit by producing standards documents for the teaching of science, history, geography, English, and foreign languages. Standards have been created to guide teacher education as well. The International Society for Technology in Education (ISTE) has produced a set of standards related to what teachers should know and be able to do concerning technology (Thomas, et al., 1997). The set of standards that is meant to apply to *all* teachers is reproduced in Figure 1–1.

Educational funding agencies, particularly the National Science Foundation, began to make use of these new standards in distributing grants. Programs that referenced these standards, and programs that encouraged *systemic* change, were the recipients of funds. State departments of education, through these funding channels, were encouraged to develop standards-based curriculum improvement projects. A major requirement of any funded curriculum improvement

---

FOUNDATION IN TECHNOLOGY FOR ALL TEACHERS

I. Foundations.   The ISTE Foundation Standards reflect professional studies in education that provide fundamental concepts and skills for applying information technology in educational settings. All candidates seeking initial certification or endorsements in teacher preparation programs should have opportunities to meet the educational technology foundations standards.

A. Basic Computer/Technology Operations and Concepts.   Candidates will use computer systems to run software; to access, generate, and manipulate data; and to publish results. They will also evaluate performance of hardware and software components of computer systems and apply basic troubleshooting strategies as needed.

   1. operate a multimedia computer system with related peripheral devices to successfully install and use a variety of software packages.
   2. use terminology related to computers and technology appropriately in written and oral communications.
   3. describe and implement basic troubleshooting techniques for multimedia computer systems with related peripheral devices.
   4. use imaging devices such as scanners, digital cameras, and/or video cameras with computer systems and software.
   5. demonstrate knowledge of uses of computers and technology in business, industry, & society.

B. Personal and Professional Use of Technology.   Candidates will apply tools for enhancing their own professional growth and productivity. They will use technology in communicating, collaborating, conducting research, and solving problems. In addition, they will plan and participate in activities that encourage lifelong learning and will promote equitable, ethical, and legal use of computer/technology resources.

   1. use productivity tools for word processing, database management, and spreadsheet applications.
   2. apply productivity tools for creating multimedia presentations.
   3. use computer-based technologies including telecommunications to access information and enhance personal and professional productivity.
   4. use computers to support problem solving, data collection, information management, communications, presentations, and decision making.
   5. demonstrate awareness of resources for adaptive assistive devices for students with special needs.
   6. demonstrate knowledge of equity, ethics, legal, and human issues concerning use of computers and technology.
   7. identify computer and related technology resources for facilitating lifelong learning and emerging roles of the learner and the educator.
   8. observe demonstrations or uses of broadcast instruction, audio/video conferencing, and other distant learning applications.

Figure 1–1.   The ISTE Foundational Standards

Continued

C. Application of Technology in Instruction.   Candidates will apply computers and related technologies to support instruction in their grade level and subject areas. They must plan and deliver instructional units that integrate a variety of software, applications, and learning tools. Lessons developed must reflect effective grouping and assessment strategies for diverse populations.

1. explore, evaluate, and use computer/technology resources including applications, tools, educational software, and associated documentation.
2. describe current instructional principles, research, and appropriate assessment practices as related to the use of computers and technology resources in the curriculum.
3. design, deliver, and assess student learning activities that integrate computers/ technology for a variety of student grouping strategies and for diverse student populations.
4. design student learning activities that foster equitable, ethical, and legal use of technology by students.
5. practice responsible, ethical, and legal use of technology, information, and software resources.

The *Curriculum Guidelines for Accreditation of Educational Computing and Technology Programs* document is available from ISTE. Order number—1-800-336-5191.

Figure 1–1.   *Continued*

project was assessment. Therefore, new means of assessing learning in these new curricula were developed. Projects that had a technology element were especially favored in many of the funding programs. Since these funding sources were most often federal monies, and since the standards were being produced by *national* councils of subject area experts, one of the effects has been a move toward more uniformity of curriculum from state-to-state. Some leaders have recommended, and some have feared, the development of a national curriculum and a national program of testing.

It is not just funding agencies that have begun to make use of national standards. Program accreditation agencies have begun to use national standards in granting program accreditation. Recent guidelines from the National Council for Accreditation of Teacher Education (NCATE) include the ISTE National Standards for Technology in Teacher Preparation. This means that any school of education that desires NCATE approval *must* demonstrate that these technology standards are being met in their programs. Since a growing number of state education departments are *requiring* NCATE accreditation for their teacher education institutions, we can expect that these standards will define the expected level of technology performance for beginning teachers throughout the United States.

Meanwhile one of the hallmarks of the Clinton administration has been a commitment to bringing the resources of the Internet to our nation's classrooms. A major theme of the 1996 Presidential campaign was the "bridge to the future," which implied a generous use of technology in the classroom. Clinton's State-of-the-Union Address of 1997 specifically called for placing a computer in every home and an Internet connection in every school. Federal Communication Commission legislation that was approved in 1997 promised funding assistance of up to 90 percent for schools to become connected to the Internet. In the private sector, "Net Day" has become an annual event in which volunteers spend a day installing wiring and equipment in schools to bring them access to the Internet.

What Are the Technologies?

At the same time these educational and political developments were taking place, the world of electronic technology was developing at breakneck speed. Three areas of technology that directly affect education were developing rapidly: computers, multimedia, and the information infrastructure (i.e., superhighway*). For many years the effects of these technologies on the classroom were marginal. However, in recent years, due to a combination of the developing information infrastructure and the development of standards-based curricula, the impact of technology is beginning to have a profound effect on schooling.

Computers

The personal computer is the primary technological development in the last part of the twentieth century. The other major technologies are dependent on the development of the computer. Without the computer, multimedia would be primitive at best; without the computer, today's communications technologies could not exist. Al-

---

* I follow the recommendation of Chris Dede (O'Neil, 1995), who prefers the use of "information infrastructure" to "information superhighway." The problem with "superhighway" is that it merely implies increasing the volume and flow of traffic. Today's technologies should enable us to do more than just increase the flow of information.

though the three areas of technology are overlapping and interconnected, the central element for them all is the personal computer.

Multimedia

The ability to place text, sound, photographs, visual documents, and full-motion video into digital form that is read by, stored by, and reproduced by computers has led to a revolution in the way we handle these media. Since the computer can now process all these different forms of information, it is inevitable that they all are being used within a single session of communication. Strictly speaking, *multi-media* (the use of multiple forms of media in a presentation) has been available for decades. In practical terms, an abundance of multimedia presentations, including encyclopedias that contain sounds and video, has not been a reality until recently.

Communications and the Information Infrastructure

The third leg of the technology tripod is the information infrastructure. This topic is so comprehensive that we devote an entire chapter of this text to it (chapter 3), but let us introduce and define this element here. The Internet, and in particular the World Wide Web, is the single most important development in educational technology in perhaps the history of the world. The implications of this technology are so profound that it may take generations before its full impact is felt. The Internet permits previously unheard-of levels of multimedia information storage and retrieval by anyone with the technology and the skills to access it. It permits instant and/or asynchronous (occurring at disconnected times) global communications between individuals and groups. While the technologies themselves are impressive, the most significant aspect of the information infrastructure is social rather than technical. With these new communications tools, human beings are developing levels of social interaction in ways that we have yet to fully appreciate. The ultimate impact of this on schooling is unknown. Some futurists, such as Lewis Perelman (Gandolfo, 1993), have suggested that this technology will mean the rapid dismantling of schooling as we know it. Less radically, others (Gandolfo, 1993) have suggested that profound changes are taking place in our schools, partly as a result of the communication infrastructure.

HOW DID WE GET TO WHERE WE ARE NOW?

The Classroom Computer: 1980–1985

Although forward-looking teachers found ways to engage their pupils with computers prior to 1980, it was the advent of the commercially produced desktop computer that began the current era of computers in the classroom. The earliest days of this era saw the Radio Shack TRS-80 and the Apple II computers as they made their entry into the classroom. (Both of these computers can now be seen in the Smithsonian Institution's computer collection.) These computers had limited capabilities, and they were not easy to use. In general only the technically minded teacher would take the time and trouble to learn to use them and then teach children how to use them. Educational software, as such, was almost non-existent at first. The earliest educational software used the computer as an electronic flashcard or an electronic page-turner. Some notable exceptions to this were titles produced by MECC (Minnesota Educational Computing Consortium), one of the first organizations devoted to developing high-quality educational software. Some of the best early software was simulation software in which learners played a decision-making role in a scenario modeled by the computer. Computer displays were almost entirely text-based; user choices were indicated by selecting from a numbered menu. One computer that briefly challenged the status quo was the Texas Instruments 99-4A. This computer provided a brightly colored, graphical display screen and sophisticated, user-friendly software. Unfortunately, a combination of marketing errors and erroneous perceptions among the technically elite caused Texas Instruments to cease production of this computer.

During this period of time the computer itself was often the topic of study in schools. In a very real sense, the computer was viewed as a new school subject to be added to the existing curriculum. Courses in "computer literacy" were developed and offered to learners of all ages. The content of such courses often included computer programming in the BASIC language. BASIC had a small vocabulary, but it had little power. Even very simple tasks, such as programming the computer to ask and respond to a series of questions, took a considerable amount of coding effort. Another topic of study in these early computer literacy courses was the binary code* used by computers at their most fundamental levels.

During the early part of this period only a very few schools had a computer. Outside of schools, however, the business community was beginning to realize the economic benefits of computerizing their operations. Enough attention was being given to computers in American society that curriculum planners and educational leaders began to talk about the importance of including computers in schools. By the mid-1980s many schools were beginning to budget for their first large-scale computer purchases. These plans generally did not include adequate money for computer maintenance or for teacher training. In general, the schools who were planning for computers were trying to place one computer in each classroom or to provide a computer lab for students to receive the necessary training about computers.

The period 1980 to 1985 was marked by a great deal of naiveté in education. We realized that computers needed to become a part of education, but we had to define what their role was going to be. In our earliest efforts at defining their role we made the computer a topic of study, and gave it some limited responsibilities as a manager of drill material. We made beginning attempts to use the computer for teaching new material, such as through the use of computer simulations. We pursued a number of different ideas for computer-to-student ratios. Some schools wanted one computer per classroom. Others wanted computer labs. For many, the dream was to try to obtain a computer for each student. None of these arrangements was driven by clear educational mandates. An abundance of questions arose. With one computer per classroom, how would the computer be used? Would the children take turns using the computer? What would everyone else do while one child used the computer? How would the child at the computer learn the material (s)he missed while (s)he was there? With a computer lab, would each class have a session in the lab once per week? What

---

* Binary code uses a base-2 number system in which every number is converted to a string of ones and zeros. Computers read these ones and zeros as power off or power on, the only conditions that can be detected by electronic devices. All higher-level programming is ultimately converted to this level in order for the computer to operate.

would be taught in the lab? Would the lessons be taught by the class-room teacher or by a computer specialist? Did schools need to hire a computer specialist? With the computer-for-every-child model, when would the children use the computers, and what would they use them for? Where would all the computers be plugged in? How would the children divide their attention between what the teacher was saying and what was on the screen? Would we even need teachers any more? These questions and others were unresolved as educators moved into the mid-1980s.

Macintosh and the PCs: 1985–1995

In 1984 Apple introduced a startling new computer, the Macintosh. The Macintosh was marketed as "the computer for the rest of us." Apple made a major campaign out of the fact that computers, up to that point, had been difficult to learn to use. Until the Macintosh was introduced, a would-be computer user had to learn a vocabulary of text commands that had to be entered into the computer by typing. The Macintosh employed the now-familiar point-and-click technol-ogy that made use of a mouse and graphical objects on the screen. The sophistication of the Macintosh was immediately evident to anyone who knew the computers of that day. A great deal of com-puting power was required to create an easy-to-use human inter-face. At the same time, those with little or no technical background recognized that here was a computer that could be put to use almost immediately. There was a very small learning curve, and the learn-ing that was required was very intuitive. Schools, who had already been Apple's largest market with earlier computers, found the Mac-intosh to be ideal for educational applications. Educational software developers created hundreds of software titles for the "Mac."

Meanwhile IBM developed its own "Personal Computer." This "PC"* had a very different architecture and a very different audi-ence than did the Macintosh. The PC was designed for scientists and business people, an audience that found it worthwhile to invest the necessary time in learning to use the system. The earliest PCs re-lied on an operating system known as the Disk Operating System

---

* Although, strictly speaking, a Macintosh is a personal computer, the term "PC" has come to be used only in reference to IBM and IBM clone computers.

(DOS). In order to use DOS the user had to learn a number of indispensable keywords and/or keystrokes. It is important to note that at this time there was no compatibility between the Macintosh operating system and DOS. Materials created on one platform could not be used on the other. Commands learned on one platform were of no help on the other. Two distinct computing communities began to develop, and the rivalry between the two was not insignificant. Schools were most often firmly in the Apple camp.

IBM made a crucial business decision that set it apart from Apple. IBM "opened" the design of the PC to competitors. This meant that other companies (Tandy, Compaq, Toshiba, and others) could create IBM "clones." These were machines made by the other manufacturers, but which worked almost exactly like the more-expensive IBM machine. Apple specifically chose to keep the Macintosh architecture protected. Apple was the only company who could legally make a Macintosh or anything like a Macintosh.

In the early 1990s the Microsoft Company developed an operating system known as Windows for use on a PC. The Windows operating system had the "look and feel" of the graphical Macintosh operating system. At first, a user who installed Windows found that it made the PC operate more slowly, and it required an upgrade of the PC hardware. Older DOS machines were not made for Windows, and the installation of this operating system was unimpressive. The next generation of PCs, however, was powerful enough that a Windows operating system made a noticeable improvement. PCs were beginning to look and act more like the Macintosh.

Apple challenged Microsoft's Windows operating system in court claiming that Microsoft had violated Apple's rights to the Macintosh operating system. After a very long (years) and expensive court case, Apple lost the case, and Microsoft was permitted to continue to use and develop its Windows operating system. Through some very competitive marketing strategies Microsoft succeeded in selling its Windows operating system to most major manufacturers of PCs so that when consumers bought a PC they were also purchasing a pre-installed Windows operating system. Windows 95 was a major improvement on the operating system, and the PC hardware that was introduced in 1995 was able to make even better use of this operating system. Since this time the distinctions between the use of a PC and the use of a Macintosh have been subtle.

In recent years IBM and Apple have collaborated on a project that has made the two platforms more compatible. Now, disks created on a PC can be read by a Macintosh. Software written for a PC can be used on specially equipped Macintoshes. Data and documents created in one platform can be read by the other. Sharing of software and data between these platforms has improved, but it is still not seamless.

Until the watershed year of 1995 teachers could expect to find almost exclusively Apple II and Macintosh computers in schools. Today, for a variety of reasons, this situation has changed. Today's teachers need to be skillful in operating a graphical interface computer, whether it is Windows-based or Macintosh. Fortunately, skill with one platform translates easily into skill with the other.

The period of 1985 to 1995 was in many ways a time of maturing and consolidation regarding computers in education. Many schools were discovering that having children take turns using one computer led to complications and problems. The educational benefits of this type of computer use turned out to be disappointing. The use of computer labs, while successful in a limited way, turned out to have severe shortcomings. In most cases the use of a lab created a separation between the classroom curriculum and a "computer curriculum." Children were learning *about* computers in the labs, but this was at the expense of valuable learning time lost from the regular classroom. Furthermore, since computers were becoming easier to use, it became clear that courses in computer literacy were of questionable value. It became clear that not everyone needed to learn how to program a computer in BASIC.

An idea that began to evolve during this period was the idea of using the computer as an integral part of teaching the "regular" curriculum. Schools would place four or five computers into a classroom, and the teacher would use those computers as one of the tools in helping children develop concepts, conduct research, and make presentations. With four or five computers, teachers could assign half of the class to work in pairs at the computer while (s)he worked directly with the other half of the class. After a period of time, the students could rotate. This scheduling arrangement allowed the teacher much flexibility, and it made optimal use of both human and electronic resources. Researchers discovered that the educational benefits of computers were as strong when the computer was shared by two or three students as when the computer was used by a single student. In some ways, the social interaction that was generated by this arrangement enhanced learning in ways that a different arrangement could not do. Teachers discovered the great benefits of using computer databases (see chapter 5), spreadsheets (see chapter 5), and word processors (see chapter 4) in their teaching.

Another idea that became popular in some schools was the idea of using one computer in the classroom, but using it in more efficient ways than had been the case previously. Dockterman (1997) describes the "one-computer classroom" as a place in which the teacher uses the computer to "manage responsibilities and paperwork, make dazzling presentations, lead incredible discussions, manage dynamic cooperative learning activities, and inspire enlightening self-discovery" (p. 22). In Dockterman's view, the one-computer classroom is the ideal rather than a compromise.

The World Wide Web: 1995–the present

As the reader will note in chapter 3, the Internet has a history that dates to the 1960s. However, the World Wide Web, a particular component of the Internet, is a much more recent phenomenon. The World Wide Web is the graphically oriented component of the Internet that is known for "home page" presentations. It is the World Wide Web with its multimedia capabilities and ease-of-navigation that has caught the imagination of so many people around the world. Users gain access to the World Wide Web through software known as a browser. In the early 1990s, Mosaic, the world's first graphically oriented commercial browser software, became available. Shortly thereafter, the Netscape Company was formed, and Netscape Navigator began its dominance of the graphical browser market. Microsoft followed a few years later with its Internet Explorer browser. With such easy-to-use software available, the public became aware of the World Wide Web in record numbers. It wasn't long before it seemed as if everyone was talking about the Internet, the World Wide Web, and the "information superhighway." We estimate that sometime in 1995 a critical mass of Internet users was reached, and this resource became a household word in the communications/telecommunications landscape.

One major feature of the World Wide Web that makes it valuable to educators is the fact that it functions as a huge database (see chapter 5). Information and resources (lesson plans, video clips, sound clips, photographs, games, etc.) are readily available to the teacher who knows how to find them. Text documents and other forms of media are available to be downloaded from remote sites to the teacher's own computer. For example, NASA makes available recent photographs taken from the Hubble telescope (http://oposite.stsci.edu/pubinfo/Recent.html). These photographs are published along with short explanations of what the photographs depict and how the scientists interpret them. Since the Hubble is constantly providing new views of space, the recent images are always changing. This is an example of the kind of educational resource that can be found on the web.

Beyond the fact that the web provides a resource of teaching materials it serves as a way of bringing people together. Teachers can join mailing lists devoted to special interests that they have. Through this means they can engage in idea-sharing with peers from around the world. This is one way in which the isolation of the teaching profession is being broken. Also, children can engage in controlled exchanges of information with other children from around the world. Many organizations have been formed to allow classrooms from around the world to engage in Internet projects together.

WHERE ARE WE NOW?

Numbers and Types of Computers

After almost 20 years of computers in the classroom, where do our classrooms stand today in terms of the numbers and types of computers? The answer to this question has a great deal to do with where you look. On one hand the picture is very encouraging: virtually all of our schools have computers. In this regard we appear to be in better condition than other developed countries. According to data from World Media Project, 1993, (quoted in Gandolfo, 1993), the United States has fewer students per computer (13) than Sweden (21), the United Kingdom (25), Germany (50), or France (60–70). The misleading aspect of these numbers, however, is that they do not expose the disparity between affluent schools and disadvantaged schools. While affluent and disadvantaged schools both have computers, the kinds of computers they have, the condition they are in, and the uses that are made of those computers are vastly different.

Affluent schools tend to have the newest or nearly newest models of computers; disadvantaged schools have outdated models. Affluent schools tend to have budgets and staff devoted to maintenance. Disadvantaged schools tend to have no technical support; when their computers break down they remain unusable. Affluent schools tend to attract teachers who have technical training, or they provide such training to their teachers through in-service training opportunities. Disadvantaged schools tend to have to settle for teachers without much technical background, and they tend not to provide much in-service technical training. At the close of the twentieth century one our our great problems is the growing gap between the technological "haves" and "have-nots" in our public school system (Piller, 1992).

Skills of Teachers

Courses in educational computing as a part of teacher-preparation programs are not new. During the 1980s, when computers were making their earliest entrance into the schools, courses in educational computing also entered the teacher-preparation program. However, just as the focus of educational computing was itself undergoing an evolution in the 1980s and 1990s, the content of these courses has undergone a similar evolution. That evolution continues today. Not only has the content of educational computing courses undergone changes, but the quality and existence of educational computing courses has varied widely from one institution to another. These factors have led to a situation in which there is great variability in terms of the technology skills possessed by today's teachers.

Many teachers who have been teaching 15 to 20 years or more have taken the initiative to learn and to keep abreast of computer technology skills. In most cases these teachers have been leaders in terms of bringing technology into the schools. Many other teachers have accepted the presence of technology, but have been unable to see how it could dramatically change what goes on in the classroom. Still others have actively resisted the arrival of technology in the classroom. All three types of teachers work side-by-side in today's schools. Newly prepared teachers, whose preparation will be affected by the *National Standards for Educational Technology* (Thomas, et al., 1997), will enter the profession with yet another perspective.

Currently teachers need skills with productivity tools (word processing, spreadsheets, and databases) and they need to be able to integrate technology into the curriculum. In addition to this they need to be able to find, evaluate, and select specific educational software that will enhance learning in the various subject areas. Finally they must be able to use the Internet and World Wide Web as teaching resources.

Uses of Technology

The ways in which teachers use technology are as varied as the teachers themselves. The philosophy of the teacher and/or the school district will profoundly influence the way in which technology is used. Philosophically teachers tend to fall along a continuum ranging from highly behaviorist on one hand to radically constructivist on the other. Teachers who are more behaviorist will favor uses of technology that allow them to more effectively manage the individual learning of skills and objectives. Teachers who are more constructivist will prefer uses of technology that permit students to explore and investigate areas of knowledge. Figure 1–2 illustrates a range of uses of technology along with a philosophical continuum ranging from behaviorist to constructivist. Chapters 6 through 9 discuss specific uses of technology in various subject areas of the curriculum. Some general principles about types of software are presented here.

Constructivist Educational Software

Software that permits the learner to take control and explore questions of particular interest to himself or herself would be compatible

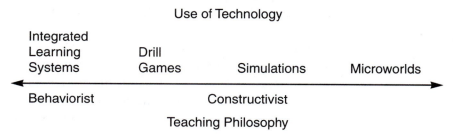

Figure 1–2.   **Uses of Technology**

with a constructivist philosophy of teaching. There is a wide variety of software that fits this criteria. In general, software that is built on the principles of hyperlinks allows students to follow links from one node of information to another according to their own individual interests and purpose. (Hypermedia and the related vocabulary, including hyperlinks, are explained fully in chapter 3.) Much of the software that is in this category allows the learner to create multimedia presentations as well. A typical use of this kind of software is as follows:

1. Allow the student to engage in a little free exploration.

2. Have the student pose a problem or define a question to be pursued.

3. Guide the student in finding the resources to answer the question or solve the problem.

4. Help the student create a multimedia presentation to be used for sharing about the problem with others.

5. Provide a forum for students to share their multimedia presentations.

In general, software that is appropriate for a constructivist teaching philosophy is not intended as "stand-alone" software. That is, unless it is in the hands of a skillful, constructivist teacher, it offers little educational value. A constructivist teacher will use this software as part of a carefully designed learning experience for her students. Most students, if left to themselves with software of this sort, will be frustrated by a lack of structure. The structuring of the learning experience comes from the interaction between the teacher and the student; it is not resident in the software itself.

Simulations

A type of software that provides more built-in structure for learning is simulation software. A simulation uses technology to model some aspect or event in the real world. This model is then used by the learner to gain some knowledge or skill that is to be transferred to the real world. Simulations are available mostly in science and social studies to assist in teaching about a variety of topics. Simulations are appropriate where certain practical considerations like cost or safety or size or time make it undesirable for the students to engage in the real-world activities. In a typical simulation the learner must make decisions, enter those decisions into the computer, and receive feedback from the computer regarding the outcomes of those decisions.

Drill Games

Some aspects of learning require students to commit things to memory. Most children find it necessary to rehearse (drill) this kind of information in order to memorize it. Games can be an effective way to provide this drill, and computer games are sometimes particularly effective.

A typical example is a game in which children are shooting invading space aliens. Each alien has an addition (or multiplication, or subtraction, or division) fact, and the "gun" has an answer to an addition fact. The child must aim the gun at the matching fact and shoot the appropriate alien. As the child's recall of the arithmetic facts becomes more automatic, the score (s)he can obtain in the game increases. A large number of different games are available for drill in many areas of the curriculum.

Integrated Learning Systems

An Integrated Learning System (ILS) is a sophisticated package of software that allows teachers to provide individualized tutoring and practice to their students. Some integrated learning systems are keyed to particular textbooks so that the teacher can coordinate the students' use of the system as a support to the textbook lessons. In most ILSs the software responds to the answers given by the student and provides customized instruction on the basis of those responses. If a child shows mastery at a particular level the software automatically increases the difficulty level. If a child shows particular patterns of errors, the software provides tutoring that is appropriate to those errors. While the student is working at the computer the computer is keeping track of her responses and scores. The teacher can later gain access to the student's scores in order to manage and interpret the work the student has done. An ILS that is built on this model will appeal to a teacher with a behaviorist philosophy.

Other ILS software has been developed on a more constructivist foundation, but this is not the normal philosophical orientation of an ILS.

Internet Projects

One of the strengths of the Internet for education is its use for bringing people together. Internet projects can be used for this purpose. In general an Internet project attempts to bring together people whose distance from one another can be used as an asset. People who are geographically separated to the extent that they have different climates would be good partners for an Internet project focused on weather and climate. People who live in different countries would be appropriate partners for projects focused on currency or culture or language differences, for example. It would not be particularly appropriate to develop an Internet project in which the distant participants were all alike in significant ways. The aspect of geographical separation should be turned into an asset for Internet projects.

In one model of Internet projects a teacher puts out an announcement for an upcoming project and asks for collaborators. Potential collaborators e-mail the coordinator offering to participate. This project coordinator then selects a team of 6 to 8 participating classrooms. These classrooms conduct local research, often including local data collection. The data are then shared with all the participants, and an analysis is conducted. Finally, a concluding report or project is published on-line, and all participants receive hard copies. Projects can be interdisciplinary, or they can be focused on science, geography, literature, history, language, or even mathematics. Most Internet projects last for a period of several weeks, and they usually comprise a small to moderate percentage of the total educational activities of the classes involved. Occasionally a creative teacher will integrate an Internet project into every subject area she teaches, and in so doing she makes the Internet project a very major part of the total curriculum. This is not required in order for an Internet project to be a success, however.

Internet Field Trips

Another use of the Internet for education is the use of the Internet for virtual field trips. In this case a group of scientists undertakes an expedition and shares enough aspects of this expedition on-line so that schools can actually participate in the expedition as it is occurring. NASA has sponsored a number of such "field trips," including trips to Antarctica, Mars, and Jupiter. (The Mars and Jupiter trips have the students participating with the team of scientists directing the unmanned space probes to those planets.) With these field trips the classes join a listserv where updates on the expedition are published regularly. Students are encouraged to send e-mail questions to the scientists who then select questions to answer. NASA provides a web-site to accompany each trip, and many teaching resources are made available to teachers who are using the trip in their classes. Unit plans, lesson plans, activities, and project ideas are all part of the available resources.

Local Variability

The ways in which technology is used in schools depends largely on the socio-economic condition of the school. Schools in disadvantaged areas, in keeping with their other characteristics regarding technology, tend to use their computers for lower-level cognitive functions than do schools in affluent areas. Disadvantaged schools use the computer for individual students, and they tend to use them for drill and games. Affluent schools tend to use software that encourages problem solving, exploration of concepts, and the construction of multimedia presentations. Affluent schools are less likely to place individual students in front of the computer and are more likely to have computers used by small groups of students.

CONCLUSION

Technology is a major part of the reform agenda for American schools today. The field of educational computing has matured over the last 20 years. Instead of viewing computers as a specific topic of study, we now realize that computers can enhance and change the way school subjects are taught. Computer tools can be integrated into every area of the school curriculum. In the next chapter we will begin to consider how computers and other technologies might actually *change* the way children learn and think about school subjects.

THINK ABOUT

- What will happen if some schools succeed in using technology to enhance teaching and others fail? Describe the future for the children who attend each kind of school.

- Some teachers resist technology in education because they can't see immediate benefits to children when technology is introduced. Should such teachers be forced to embrace technology? What are some of the implications of your answer to this question?

- A competitive marketplace in America has contributed to computers becoming easier to use since the 1980s. What are some of the limitations and weaknesses of today's technologies? How might competition in the marketplace work to overcome some of these limitations?

- Are some of the educational uses of technology described in this chapter better than others? What makes one use of technology better than another? Develop an evaluation rubric that you can use to evaluate educational uses of technology.

SELECTED REFERENCES

Branscum, D. (1992). "Educators need support to make computing meaningful." *Macworld* (September), 83–88.

Dockterman, D. (1997). *Great teaching in the one computer classroom* (4th ed.). Watertown, MA: Tom Snyder Productions.

Gandolfo, R. (1993). "Will technology alter traditional teaching?" *Christian Science Monitor* (September 22), 9, 12.

National Council of Teachers of Mathematics (1989). *Curriculum and evaluation standards for school mathematics.* Reston, VA: National Council of Teachers of Mathematics.

O'Neil, J. (1995). "On technology and schools: A conversation with Chris Dede." *Educational Leadership* (October), 6–12.

Piller, C. (1992). "Separate realities." *Macworld* (September), 218–231.

Thomas, L., Friske, J., Knezek, D., Taylor, H., and Wiebe, J. (1997). *National standards for educational technology.* International Society for Technology in Education.

Tyler-Wood, T., Putney, D., and Cass, M. (1997). "Accessibility: The main factor influencing special education teachers' perceived level of computer competence." *Journal of Computing in Teacher Education,* 13(4), 20–24.

2 The Delta Principle

LOOKING AHEAD

"I don't see what all the fuss is about computers. I've been teaching long enough that I've seen this before. First it was the movie projector that was going to 'transform' education. Then it was the filmstrip projector. Then it was programmed textbooks. Then it was the overhead projector. It just goes on and on. At first I believed it. Now I know better. Now I say I have yet to see anything as reliable and dependable as a piece of chalk and a chalkboard."

If you've heard teachers talking like this, you know that today's technological developments are not being received without some skepticism. There are good reasons for teachers to feel the way this teacher feels. Educational technology has an unfortunate history of having been oversold. On the other hand, there are real reasons to be very excited about the possibilities technology has to offer teachers. Although we cannot expect technology to solve all the problems that schools face, we can expect technology to change the way we do things. Sometimes those changes are anticipated, and sometimes they are not. Sometimes those changes are beneficial, and sometimes they are not.

CAN YOU?

- Define what is meant by the Delta Principle?
- Tell the difference between Levels I, II, and III of the Delta Principle?

- Give examples of inventions that have changed society?

- Give examples of some unanticipated benefits of certain inventions?

- Give examples of some unanticipated harm that has come from certain inventions?

TEACHER LABORATORY

Calculator Experiment

Do you use a calculator to balance your checkbook? Have you ever maintained a checkbook without the benefit of a calculator? Do a little investigative work (ask family members and friends) to see if you can find anyone who does not use a calculator to maintain their checkbook. *If* you can find such a person, does this person do the arithmetic, or does (s)he just take the bank's word for the balance at the end of each month? After conducting this experiment on your own, discuss the results with your classmates who tried it also. What effect has the calculator had on our checkbook habits? What are the positive and negative sides to these effects? What implications does this have for our teaching of elementary arithmetic?

Telephone Answering Machine

Before the telephone answering machine was popular, people's telephone behaviors were different than they are today. How do you think people's telephone behaviors have changed as a result of this machine? Talk to people who have lived most of their lives without a telephone answering machine but who now use one. Find out their opinions about how this machine has changed things for the better and for the worse. If you can, find someone who *refuses* to get an answering machine. Find out why this person refuses to have one of these machines. Compare what you found out with what your classmates found out. What do your discoveries have to do with educational technology? Revisit this Teacher Laboratory *after* you have read this chapter.

THE DELTA PRINCIPLE DEFINED

In order to understand and appreciate the potential of technology to transform education we need to explore a general principle concerning the effects of technology. For the purposes of this exploration, technology will be examined first in a general way in order to deduce an important principle. Then, once the principle is defined, we will illustrate it in a few ways to show how it operates with various technologies. Finally, we'll discuss why this principle is important to consider in the more narrow context of technology and education. The principle that we are developing will be called the Delta Principle after the Greek *delta,* meaning change.

Simply stated, our assertion is that any invention can be effective in changing the way humans live. When a human makes an invention it is normally in response to a difficulty that has occurred in an attempt to accomplish a specific task. At first the invention is used to overcome that specific difficulty for that specific task. The user of the invention is able to accomplish that initial task either more quickly or more efficiently than was possible previously. An example of this might be the original use of the telephone to allow people to talk together over large distances. Use of an invention at this stage represents Level I of the Delta Principle. In reference to educational technology, Maddux, et al. (1997) refer to this as "Type I" applications of technology. They assert that such applications of technology make it "easier, quicker, or otherwise more efficient to continue teaching the same things in the same ways we have always taught them" (p. 18).

After a time the user of the invention may find that it can be applied to different tasks other than the one for which it was invented. This represents an expansion of the role of the invention into areas the inventor either didn't think of or thought of only in a secondary way. Continuing the example of the telephone, people began to discover that it could be useful as a tool in conducting opinion surveys. Others began to realize that it had potential as a marketing tool. Still others began to explore the possibility of the telephone system carrying electronic data signals instead of just the human voice. When an invention is applied to uses beyond that for which it was originally intended, this represents Level II of the Delta Principle.

Level II is a transitionary level in the use of the invention. The expansion of the use of the invention into new areas may lead to the development of new kinds of tasks that were not possible without the invention. These are tasks that are dependent on the invention for their very existence. The idea of an election outcome being affected by polling data collected and reported in the weeks preceding the election is dependent on telephone technology. The ability to carry on a conversation via e-mail with a person with whom your schedule never coincides is dependent in many cases on telephone lines to carry the messages. When tasks are being carried out that are dependent on an invention, this represents Level III of the Delta Principle. It is at this point that we can say that the invention has changed the way people live. In reference to educational technology, Maddux, et al. (1997) refer to such applications of technology as "Type II." Simply stated, they assert that such applications "make available new and better ways of teaching" (p. 18).

Level III of the Delta Principle is very profound. The activities that characterize this level are activities that would not exist without the technology. If, somehow, the technology would cease to exist, the activities of Level III would also cease to exist. For a time, perhaps, people would try to find alternative ways to do the tasks that the technology had enabled them to do, but these attempts would be doomed to failure. Without the technology, Level III activities would require more effort as input than could be justified on the basis of the results. Without telephones, national opinion surveys could only be conducted with a huge corps of workers and an excellent transportation system. Hundreds of workers all over the country would have to simultaneously poll people in their region using a standardized questionnaire. Then these workers would need to air-mail their findings to a central location for processing. The costs of such a procedure would be prohibitive. Therefore, although they theoretically *could* be conducted without telephones, national opinion surveys *would* not exist without the technology of the telephone. Therefore, the modern notion of political campaigns being shaped by public opinion polls owes its existence to telephone technology.

To compare this to Level I tasks: Level I tasks were being done before the invention existed, albeit, they were being done more slowly or less efficiently. Without the invention, the Level I tasks would still be in existence. We would revert to doing them slowly and inefficiently.

THE DELTA PRINCIPLE

Level I: Technology used as originally intended

Level II: Technology applied in new ways

Level III: Application would not exist without the technology

Figure 2–1.   The Delta Principle

THE DELTA PRINCIPLE ILLUSTRATED

Since the Delta Principle is so general, it can be illustrated in a number of different contexts. By examining this principle in many contexts the reader will gain a deep understanding of it. Beginning with an example that is not from the field of education, we will here illustrate the Delta Principle in relation to automobiles, printed books, and calculators.

Automobiles

The first automobiles were conceived of as "horseless carriages." At the time of their invention most people lived in small towns or cities. Distances that people could travel easily were limited. Communities provided most of the goods and services that people needed within a short distance from their homes. "Roads" were dirt or stone pathways. At Level I of their use, automobiles were intended to make travel faster and easier. (In the case of automobiles there evidently was a time when travel by automobile was more difficult than the alternatives, as evidenced by the phrase "get a horse.")

As automobiles became popular, they permitted changes to be made in people's lifestyles. Whereas previously people needed to live very close to their places of work and their sources of goods and services, the automobile permitted them to live further away from these essentials of life. The communities hadn't changed, with the exception that people now were able to live further away from the community centers. This stage in the relationship between the automobile and the community might be referred to as an example of Level II of the Delta Principle.

Eventually the sources of employment and goods and services also relocated from community centers. This shift was made possible because of the ability of people to travel greater distances. Today's suburban neighborhoods have virtually no employment and no goods or services located within walking distance of homes. An automobile is now essential for life in the suburbs. The dependency of the suburban way of life on the automobile represents Level III of the Delta Principle.

The Printed Word

Before the printing press, books were relatively rare. The ancient library at Alexandria, Egypt contained about 250,000 volumes of the world's collected knowledge. This library was the only one of its magnitude in the world. Most people could not read or write. People depended heavily on oral language for their learning. Books had to be copied by hand or set in type that could not be changed once it had been set.

Gutenburg intended the invention of moveable type to make the production of books faster, cheaper, and easier. At Level I of the Delta Principle, books could proliferate, but at first few people needed them.

Near the same time, the early Protestant Christian leaders began to encourage common people to read and respond to the Bible. (This was in contrast to traditional Roman Catholic teaching which had attempted to prevent private interpretation and misuse of the Bible by designating priests as the official interpreters. At the time, priests were often the only members of a community who knew how to read.) Because books could be produced relatively cheaply and abundantly, more and more Bibles were made available for common people. With the availability of Bibles came an increased need for reading education. Books (and reading) began to play an expanded role in the lives of everyday people. A primary expanded role was that the Bible provided a religious message to common people, and they responded to it personally, without relying on priests as official interpreters. This in itself changed history, as it helped to spark the Protestant Reformation.

Eventually the role of books expanded greatly, to the point where today the printed word touches every area of life. Instruction (formal and informal), entertainment, current events, legal transactions, and financial transactions are totally dependent on the printed word. Although we cannot prove that it is true, it seems likely that people's ability to remember oral language is much less today than it was before printed books were popular. Whereas there once was a time when people *could* learn by oral tradition, that day seems to have disappeared. Reading is recognized to be the single most important of the various school subjects. Without an ability to read, a person in our society is severely handicapped. The use of the printed word has reached Level III of the Delta Principle.

To illustrate how it is that the Delta Principle affects education, consider the whole language method of teaching reading. Abundant, inexpensive, paperback trade books that are designed for children of all ages are a relatively recent phenomenon. The success of the whole language method of teaching reading is dependent on the abundance of such trade books. Children are supposed to be "immersed in literature." Such immersion is not possible without an abundance of good literature available to the children. Prior to the availability of inexpensive, paperback trade books for children, beginning reading instruction centered heavily on instruction in phonics and on controlled vocabulary. Basal readers, an essential educational technology of an earlier time, were a necessity in a world that lacked abundant, available children's literature.

Abundant, available children's literature was not designed in order to facilitate whole language reading instruction. Rather, this method of teaching reading grew out of an environment that was rich in children's books. The whole language method of teaching reading is a Level III result of abundant children's literature.

Electronic Cash Register

Turning to a more recent innovation in technology, we have seen the development of a dependence on electronic calculating cash registers. The technology of cash registers has changed somewhat as we've gone through Levels I, II, and III of the Delta Principle.

When the cash register was first invented its purpose was to simplify daily bookkeeping related to cash sales. It was designed to record a particular sale and add that sale to the total sales for the day. At the end of the day the amount of cash in the drawer was compared to the sum recorded by the register to ensure that no money was missing. At Level I, the machine made tallying the day's receipts easier. Since the machine did not compute the change that the customer needed for each sale, the clerk operating the machine had to do this computation mentally.

With the advent of electronic machines the role of the cash register expanded. New capabilities included the machine's ability to tell the clerk and the customer how much change was needed for each sale. At Level II, initially, both the clerk and the machine had the ability to "make change." The clerk had been trained to do so in school and through much experience. The machine had been programmed to perform this computation.

With machines that could make change it was no longer necessary for the clerk to mentally compute change with each transaction. Simultaneously, changes in the way we pay for things (credit cards, checks, debit cards, food stamps, discount coupons) led to fewer transactions in which change was required at all. Today we see store clerks who are dependent upon the electronic "cash register" to process all of the arithmetic required for every sale. We often see store clerks who appear to be unable to make change in a mental computation. Rather than seeing this as evidence of a faltering educational system, we maintain that this is evidence of the electronic cash register functioning at Level III of the Delta Principle.

EXERCISE 2–1   YOU TRY IT

Think about an invention that you use. How does your lifestyle depend in some way on that invention? What was the original intent of the invention? If the invention were to disappear, how would your life change? How has your life changed as a result of that invention? Compare your answers to answers given by your classmates.

WHY IS THE DELTA PRINCIPLE IMPORTANT?

Once we begin to view technology from the perspective of the Delta Principle we can begin to understand why this Principle is so important, especially at this time in history. We are all well aware of the dramatic technological developments that have characterized the late twentieth century. The two interrelated areas of computer technology and communications technology have seen unprecedented development in recent decades. There is no sign that the pace of these developments is slowing down. In spite of this, most people's attention seems to be focused on the technological developments themselves rather than on how these technologies might change society. When we do focus on change it is usually after the changes have begun to occur, and we often dislike the changes that we see. Often what we hear about are the unintended negative effects of technologies.

This illustrates another feature of the Delta Principle. Level III changes caused by technology can be either positive or negative in their effects. While technology enables us to do good in ways that our ancestors could only dream about (consider the benefits of advanced medical technologies), we have also created greater nightmares than they would have imagined (consider the notion of nuclear warfare). Technology functions as a multiplier of our abilities. Our ability to do good is multiplied by technology. Our capacity for harm is also multiplied by technology. One of the very simplest of simple machines, the lever, illustrates this point very well. A lever multiplies our strength. With this multiplied strength we can either remove heavy obstacles, or we can pry open a locked door to commit a robbery. The lever is not invested with either good or evil, but how we use it certainly has moral and ethical implications.

Furthermore, these positive and negative effects of technology can be either intended or unintended. With positive and negative effects, as well as intended and unintended effects, four combinations of effects are possible. (See Figure 2–2.) Generally the positive intended effects of technology are the Level I effects: the effects for which the invention was designed. The positive, unintended effects of technology are the things that we've been describing as Level III effects. These are beneficial changes brought about by an invention that the inventor couldn't have intended because they come from activities that were not possible before the existence of the invention. On the darker side, there may be inventions that have an intended negative effect. Weapons are an invention that may come to mind here. However, bear in mind that the inventor of a weapon most often probably has a positive effect in mind (protection, defense, hunting for food) when he makes the invention. Only the person or animal on which the weapon is used would see its effect as negative.

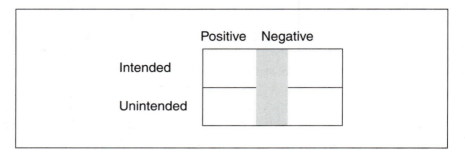

Figure 2–2.   Effects of Technology

Of much greater concern to us as educators are the unintended negative effects of technology. Many examples of this could be cited. An effect of this sort that comes from popular network television programming is an increasing need that children have for visual stimulation. Another effect of this programming is the dwindling attention span that is seen in both children and adults. There are so many examples of unintended negative effects of various technologies in our culture that many people (perhaps including some readers of this text) have become cynical about technology and its effects. For these people, their experiences with the unintended negative effects of technology have given them a resistance to technological developments. These are people who actively or passively resist the "intrusion" of technology into their lives, believing that no good can come of it.

In order to illustrate the potential positive and negative unintended effects of technology on education, we present two very different perspectives. One is from the Apple Classroom of Tomorrow (ACOT) project as reported by one of that project's directors in 1994. The other perspective comes from a more recent article in which the author compares the arrival of technology in schools with the advent of mechanization of farming.

The Apple Classroom of Tomorrow Project

In the late 1980s Apple Computer began its sponsorship of a project to explore the effects of a heavy infusion of technology into education. At initially three sites around the country, computers were provided to teachers and students for both classroom and home use. The project designers (Dwyer, 1994) anticipated that students' educational experiences would become more individualized as the teachers began to take advantage of drill-and-practice software that was abundant at the time. Furthermore, they expected that students would increase their ability to express themselves in writing due to the availability of word processing software. However, the expectations of the project directors did not drive the project; the teachers did. The interest of the project directors was to discover what effects the abundant technology might have on teaching and learning.

As the project progressed through several years, a progression of changes was noted in how children used the technology for learning and in how teachers used it for teaching. The earliest changes noted were changes in the children. By the end of the second year of the project the children were reportedly interacting more with each other than they had been previously. The children were spontaneously helping each other with projects. They were curious about one another's work even while they were excited about their own work. In the third year of the project the teachers were changing. They initiated more team-teaching, they worked more across the disciplines, and they began to rearrange the school schedule in order to accommodate needs to spend time working on extended projects. They also began to make extensive use of the technology to boost their own productivity and manage their responsibilities.

By the fourth year the teachers were beginning to design *"new kinds of tasks for students,"* (Dwyer, p. 6; italics added). They had rearranged their classrooms to accommodate to the needs of projects; they were encouraging far more collaboration among their students; they had to arrange for students to stay after school (voluntarily) to continue to work on multimedia projects. The following quote illustrates what was a true Delta Level III positive effect,

> By the time our sites were reporting new kinds of outcomes for students, we had witnessed what amounted to a transformation of their learning cultures. For example, teachers' instructional beliefs and practices underwent an evolution, and we believed the improvement in students' competencies to be a result of teachers' personal appropriation of the technology. (Dwyer, p. 9)

Where the designers of the project had anticipated more individualized learning and more use of drill-and-practice software, almost the opposite occurred. A word repeated over and over in the report of the ACOT project is "collaboration." The students became collaborators on projects and the teachers became collaborators with each other and with their students. Students and teachers collaborated together, with the students often in the role of expert or resource person. Drill-and-practice software was ignored while multimedia development software was used extensively.

The designers of the project hoped that students' test scores would be improved as a result of the use of drill-and-practice software. In fact, even though the technology was not used a great deal to directly benefit test scores, the test scores of the ACOT classrooms were at least as good as those in non-ACOT classrooms, and in some cases the ACOT children did better. Beyond the test score measurements, a four-year longitudinal study showed that the greatest difference was in how the ACOT students organized for and accomplished their work. They used a great deal of inquiry, collaborative, technological, and problem-solving skills.

The ACOT project epitomizes the Delta Principle, particularly in terms of unanticipated positive effects of technology. The technology enabled teachers to dramatically improve the learning environment in their classrooms. It also epitomizes what might be termed the "Emperor's New Clothes" perspective on technology in education. No limitations of technology are noted in the ACOT reports. No negative effects of technology are suggested in the ACOT reports. To take the ACOT reports at face value would be to accept the notion that technology is the panacea that education has been searching for for ages. Such a view is common in the literature on educational computing. It is important for educators to keep this view in check by asking critical questions and exploring the possible negative effects of technology.

The Limitations of Technology

Since there are so many things that computers and communications technologies can do, it is easy to slip into the trap of thinking that they can do *all* things well. There has perhaps never been a tool with such generalizable capabilities, many of which are explored in this text. But what are the limitations of these technologies? What are the things that these technologies cannot do well? What aspects of education might be ignored when we rely more and more on technology in education?

Lowell Monke (1997) cogently articulates the value judgments that are implied whenever we make a choice to use computers in some degree in education. Computers represent efficiency and progress. The newest generations of multimedia computers stimulate the senses of sight and sound. Computers are well-suited to tasks that require manipulation of large amounts of data. When we choose to use computers we are implicitly encouraging the values behind those strengths: efficiency, progress, sensation (of sight and sound only), and control of data. There may be nothing inherently wrong with reinforcing those values. However, at the same time, our decision to use computers leaves other values behind. Computers are notoriously bad at making judgments. They are incapable of distinguishing between truth and falsehood at anything above a purely mathematical level. They cannot identify beauty or the lack of it. Discovery of meaning is generally beyond the capabilities of computers. They cannot generate their own ideas, nor can they encourage human beings in generating their own ideas. They cannot distinguish between a great idea and a trivial fact. In general, there is an entire range of human thought and emotion (wisdom?) that is beyond the scope of technology. Since our choice to computerize education does nothing to develop the values behind this range of human thought and emotion, we run the risk of diminishing these values in future generations.

When considering this possibility we must remember that most of us have grown to maturity in an environment where computers played a very small to modest role in our development. We have been encouraged to develop into full human beings, so it may be difficult for us to imagine the kinds of human handicaps that could result from a computer-rich but human-poor educational environment. We must look beyond ourselves, however, and realize that our concern is for the next generation. Where will today's children obtain wisdom? How will they develop emotional maturity and judgment? Since computers are unable to develop these qualities it will be up to the educators to do so. When we are using such powerful tools as computers it is more important than ever before for human teachers to understand and nurture the things that only humans can do. As Monke (1997) states it, ". . . Because the computer distracts us from the pursuit of the higher goals of education, teachers who can keep focused on them become more critical," and, "It is a task that can be performed only by a caring, thoughtful person dedicated to elevating the inner life of each child" (p. 34).

CLOSING THOUGHTS

One of the reasons it is vital that we understand the Delta Principle and the positive and negative effects of technology is that by understanding these things we can begin to exercise some control over them. If we can anticipate what some unintended negative effects of a technology might be on children's learning, then we can take steps to minimize those potential negative effects. If we can imagine ways in which a technology can improve the way children think and learn, then we are in a position to help to bring about those benefits. One of the primary goals of this text is to equip the reader to anticipate and imagine these possible effects of technology on children's learning. If teachers become skilled in such thinking, then their use of technology will be of the greatest benefit to children, and the negative impacts of technology will be minimized.

Because this is a major goal of this text, we use the Delta Principle as a theme for the text. Chapters 4 through 9 each include a *Delta Principle Perspective,* which is intended to consider the material from that chapter in light of the Delta Principle. Where it is possible to do so, we provide evidence from educational research to indicate whether the desired benefits of technology are being realized in classrooms. Some of the time, however, we are using our informed imaginations to speculate about what *could* be the effects of technology: both negative and positive. Our hope is that the reader will be able to develop an ability to do this same speculation about the possible effects of technology. We believe such informed imagining will contribute to the teacher's wisdom in using technology in the classroom.

THINK ABOUT

- Consider the school bus as an educational technology. Develop a Delta Principle analysis of the school bus. Are there any Level II effects of the school bus? Are there any Level III effects? Are there both positive and negative effects of this invention? Are there intended and unintended positive and negative effects? Describe these.

- Pick another tool that is prevalent in education as you know it. Develop a Delta Principle analysis of it. Are there any Level II effects? Are there any Level III effects? Are there both positive and negative effects of this invention? Are there intended and unintended positive and negative effects? Describe these.

- Think about how education might have been before children were spending 25 or more hours a week watching television programs. Fill out the following chart describing the effects of television. What do you think the gray area in the middle of the chart means? Can you think of an example of intended or unintended effects of TV that might belong in this "gray area"?

	Positive	Negative
Intended		
Unintended		

- Can you think of a new technology which is only in the level I stage of use? Can you foresee some Level II applications for it? Really stretch your mind and try to envision Level III ramifications.

- Consider how the effects of technology change over time. When calculators first appeared there was great discussion over whether they should be allowed in schools because only rich students could afford them. Now nearly every student can have some type of calculator, but some teachers are worried because widespread calculator use has led to reduced ability to perform mental calculations. Similarly, most people cannot find a square root on paper, even though there is a fairly straightforward algorithm. Do you consider these to be serious problems or are they outweighed by the benefits of instructional use of calculators?

- What keeps some inventions from having the kinds of positive impact that they *could* have? Why is there skepticism among so many people about the likelihood that technology can change education?

- Must there *always* be unintended negative effects of technology?

SELECTED REFERENCES

Dwyer, D. (1994). "Apple classrooms of tomorrow: What we've learned." *Educational Leadership,* 51(April), 4–10.

Gilbert, S. (1996). "Making the most of a slow revolution." *Change* (March/April), 245–258.

Greenfield, P. (1984). *The developing child: Mind and media—the effects of television, video games, and computers.* Cambridge, MA: Harvard University Press. A nice review of some of the research on the impact of media on children.

Maddux, C. D., Johnson, D. L., and Willis, J. W. (1997). *Educational computing: Learning with tomorrow's technologies* (2nd ed.). Boston: Allyn & Bacon.

Monke, L. (1997). "The web & the plow: Putting the computer in its place." *Teacher Magazine* (October), 30–34.

Papert, S. (1980). *Mindstorms: Children, computers, and powerful ideas.* New York: Basic Books. An interesting exploration of some Level III effects of computers in the elementary math classroom.

Many encyclopedias (especially those on CD-ROM, such as World Book and Microsoft Encarta) have technology timelines. You may want to consider some of the inventions listed there from the point of view of the Delta Principle. (This is an excellent exercise to have your students carry out. In fact, you may want them to consider the CD-ROM encyclopedia itself as a technology to be analyzed critically.)

3 The Information Infrastructure

LOOKING AHEAD

In Rivard's (1997) short story, "The Virtual Classroom," 13-year-old Chris is a student of the future. He goes to "school" by climbing into a booth in his bedroom. He wears a full-body-suit that is wired to the booth and to the outside world. Rivard describes the booth:

> The interior of the booth was rather stark. The small walled environment was embellished with a myriad of small screens, LED indicator lights, cameras, microphones, speakers, sensors, and eyewear. (p. 40)

Chris's school experience is almost entirely *virtual*, that is, it exists only in a technology-induced imagination. He selects his "lessons" from a menu, and based on his selection he is treated to a learning experience that simulates real-life. The equipment in the booth provides the sense-stimulations, and these stimulations are given to Chris through the body suit. He is able to include virtual images of his friends in his lessons. Following a virtual lesson experience, he carries on real time audio and visual communication with the programmers who created his virtual experience.

Is this vision of the future of education a nightmare or a dream-come-true? How could we possibly experience such a dramatic change in education? Is there any reason to think that we are seeing today the seeds for such a radical, technology-based form of education?

CAN YOU?

- Explain why it is impossible for the Internet to "crash"?

- Identify three main areas of use of the Internet?

- Tell what a listserv is and how to join one?

- Describe the difference between a listserv and a newsgroup?

- Tell what an FTP session is for?

- Distinguish between the Internet and the World Wide Web?

- Conduct a World Wide Web search using the AND, OR, and NOT operators?

- Explain the difference between a *hypermedia* information source and an information source that is not hypermedia?

- Describe any Delta Level III implications of learning in a hyper-media environment?

TEACHER LABORATORY

Obtain a copy of Rivard's short story, "The Virtual Classroom." Read it and debate it with your classmates. Send e-mail to Rivard (34c5ous@ cmuvm.csv.cmich.edu) to express your opinions about the story. What is Rivard's reaction to your reaction?

THE INTERNET

Take two computers and connect them together with cabling, telephone lines, or other means, and you have created the simplest form of computer network. These two computers can then share resources: everything found on one of the computers can be made available to the other. If a third computer is connected to computer #2, then it can share information with computer #2. In this arrangement (which is highly unusual) information on computer #1 could be shared with computer #2 and then on to computer #3. If computer #2 breaks down, information from computer #1 cannot be shared with computer #3.

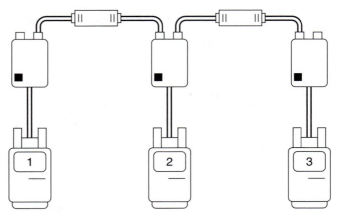

#1 shares with #2; #2 shares with #3; #3 shares with #1 indireclty through #2

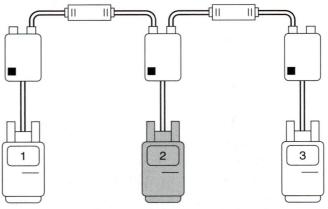

With #2 down, #3 cannot share with #1

Figure 3–1.   A Hypothetical Linear "Network"

In the late 1960s the U.S. military set up a computer network that would not be vulnerable to the destruction of a single computer in the network. In this system, which was known as ARPAnet, computers were linked in a true network, as shown in Figure 3–2. In this arrangement if any one computer fails, information can still travel between the remaining computers in the system. Furthermore, this same architecture can be extended to connect distinct networks together to create a "network of networks." Such an arrangement is shown in Figure 3–3. ARPAnet was the beginning of what is now the Internet.

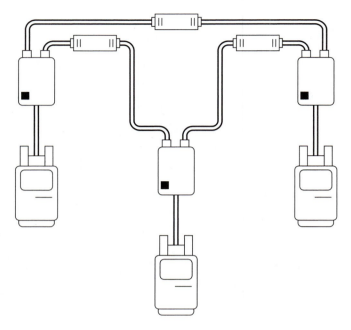

Figure 3–2.   A True Network

Most of the computers in the ARPAnet network used an operating system known as UNIX. However, one of the great accomplishments of these early networking days was the development of communications standards that would allow dissimilar machines to be added to the network. Such communications standards are known as *protocols.* The set of protocols that was developed for use in this network was known as *Transmission Control Protocol/Internet Protocol,* or TCP/IP. This standard is still the required communication protocol for today's Internet. Because of TCP/IP *any* computer that can be programmed to follow this protocol can connect to the Internet.

Although ARPAnet was the first communications network of its kind, a similar network was developed shortly afterward by the National Science Foundation. The purpose of this network, known as NSFnet, was to allow communication among academic and research institutions. In the 1980s ARPAnet and NSFnet underwent some reorganization, restructuring, and growth. The military portion became a separate network, and the academic/research portion consolidated and grew into the network now known as the Internet.

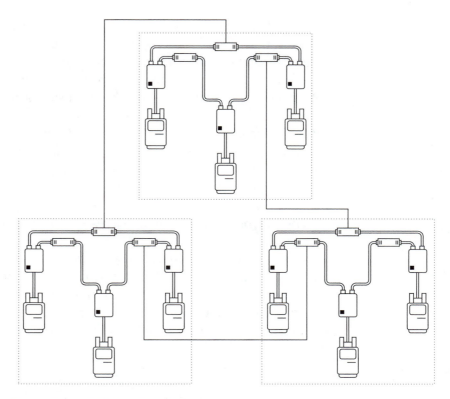

Figure 3–3.   A Network of Networks

Probably of greater importance than the physical structure of the Internet is an understanding of the various services that this network provides. Internet services can be categorized into three separate areas: communications, file-sharing, and terminal emulation. Communications services include e-mail and related services. File-sharing services allow users to download documents and software from remote locations. Terminal emulation allows users to connect to and use resources that reside on remote computers.

Communication

Communication services, in addition to e-mail, include such things as listservs and newsgroups. A listserv is a mailing list to which any member can send messages. Listservs are created to focus e-mail discussions on specific topics. An example of this for teachers might be a listserv devoted to helping children diagnosed with a particular learning disability. Any message sent to the list is received by everyone on the list. Since a message sent to a listserv usually generates several responses, and often those responses generate responses, a listserv functions as a discussion forum. The discussions usually do not take place in real time with the discussants reacting to one another "live," but rather they take place asynchronously (that is, they occur at disconnected times. I write at 8:00 AM; you read it and respond at 2:00 PM; I read your response and give my response to you at 9:00 PM). Members of the list catch up on the discussion by reading new mail messages whenever they check their mail. Some listservs are "moderated," which means that a person serves as a screener to ensure that only messages appropriate to the stated purpose of the list are posted.

Listservs are most often managed by computer software rather than by a person. After the listserv administrator creates the listserv, interested users join the list by subscribing to it. To subscribe, a person sends an e-mail message to the program that controls the list. The body of that message usually must include the command "subscribe" as well as the name of the list and the sender's e-mail address. Since this message is to be read by the computer, spelling and punctuation must be exactly correct. If the command is received and carried out by the listserv program it usually sends out an initial message to notify the user that (s)he is now subscribed to the list. At that point the new member will begin receiving messages sent to the list. If (s)he wishes to post a message to the list, (s)he again sends e-mail, this time to the list itself rather than to the program that controls the list. (In order to become a list member and then send messages to the list it is necessary to know two different addresses: one for the list program and one for the list itself.) If a time comes when the user wishes to be taken off the list it is again necessary to send an e-mail command to the program that controls the list. This time the body of the message must contain the command used to get off the list: usually the command "unsubscribe" followed by the name of the list.

It is important to know the proper command for getting off a list. Most listservs automatically send new members an e-mail message containing this important information. There is usually no way for a member to get off a list without using the appropriate command. It is considered bad etiquette (bad netiquette) to write to a list itself asking a human to take you off the list. The unsubscribe action must be taken by the member herself or himself by sending the correct command to the list-managing program.

Newsgroups serve a similar function as listservs, but they are more open. In order to participate in (or even watch) the discussion on a listserv you must send an e-mail message to subscribe. In contrast to this, anyone can "surf" into a newsgroup discussion. This freedom often results in discussions that are fragmented and that stray from the stated purpose of the newsgroup. Newsgroups are accessible directly from most web browsers. The messages posted on a newsgroup are analogous to messages posted on a public bulletin board.

Two forms of "live" communication that can have a role in classroom learning are known as "IRC" and videoconferencing. IRC stands for Internet-Relay-Chat, and it is the technology upon which "chat-rooms" are built. Although most use of chat-rooms is of dubious value to educators, the KIDLINK organization has established an IRC area specifically for children ages 10 to 15. This organization carefully monitors who uses the service (users must register with KIDLINK), and educators plan highly engaging and educational chat topics. Sometimes experts in various fields participate in the on-line dialogs, and the young people can ask questions and receive immediate answers. Videoconferencing is an extension of this same concept. Using C-U SeeMe software, which was developed at Cornell University, participants can see a small inset live video of the people involved in a chat. Users must have a video camera connected to their computer and they must have the C-U SeeMe software installed in order to participate in a video conference. As few as two or as many as 9 can participate in a video conference using C-U SeeMe. Both IRC and videoconferencing require a greater degree of technical knowledge and sophistication than some of the other Internet services described here.

File-Sharing

Another category of Internet services is file-sharing. The Internet can be used to connect to a remote database allowing you to download a copy of something stored on that database. An example of this for teachers might be connecting to the state education department to download the latest regulations or curriculum revisions. (Downloading is copying a file from a remote computer to your own.) File-sharing is used to download text, sound files, graphics, videos, and even computer software. The most common method of connection for file-sharing is called FTP, which stands for File Transfer Protocol. A connection that is made for the purpose of downloading a file is referred to as an "FTP session."

Downloading files is becoming easier all the time. Downloading that is handled through Netscape or Explorer or America Online usually can be accomplished without any special knowledge at all. (Not long ago this was not the case; it required a good deal of technical knowledge to accomplish downloading.) Files that are available for FTP transfer are often compressed to save space and transfer time. When these files arrive at the local computer they must be uncompressed. Normally the necessary software to accomplish this uncompression is already resident as a "plug-in" to the browser (Netscape or other) software. Sometimes files are downloaded that require additional plug-ins in order to be fully functional. (Sound or video files, for example, require additional plug-ins to be fully functional.) Today's browsers are equipped to notify a user of such a situation and then automatically download and install any additional plug-ins that are needed. Not long ago this process was not automated and users were often frustrated in their attempts to download special files. Today the worst part about the process is the excessive amount of time that is sometimes consumed as the computer locates and acquires the necessary plug-ins.

There are so many thousands of files available for downloading from the Internet that finding them would be impossible without some form of location tools. Where "search engines" are useful for locating home pages on the WWW, different tools are used for finding files for downloading.

Anytime a file is downloaded from the Internet there is the possibility that the file will contain a virus. A virus is a computer program written by someone who wants to cause harm to other computers. Viruses are easily attached to files that are available for downloading, and downloaded files are a common source of viruses on local computers. It is important to use virus-detection software to examine downloaded files. Virus-detection software is capable of detecting and removing most common viruses. Virus-detection software should be used before installing or using a downloaded file.

Terminal Emulation

The original ARPAnet was constructed in the days before personal computers. At that time the computing power was located in large, centralized "mainframe" computers. Users of the network had "dumb terminals" in remote locations. The terminals' only function was to serve as a window into the distant mainframe computer. Terminals had no computer processor and no computer memory. The computing took place at the mainframe; the input and output of data took place at the terminal. When personal computers began to replace terminals, the personal computers had to act like (or emulate) terminals in order to function correctly with the network. The software application that was used to make a personal computer emulate a terminal was most often the "Telnet" application. Today, occasionally, Telnet is the most efficient software to use to connect to a distant computer. Versions of Telnet are available as freeware at various sites on the Internet.

An educational example of terminal emulation would be participation in the KIDLINK IRC chat-rooms. The simplest way to participate is to use Telnet to connect to the KIDLINK IRC server, a remote computer to which a local computer connects. (Since KIDLINK is designed to be a safe environment for young people, only registered members of KIDLINK may connect to the KIDLINK IRC server.)

THE WORLD WIDE WEB

By far the most widely used and well-known Internet service is the World Wide Web (WWW). The WWW is the graphical environment composed of home pages and click-able connections from one location to another. The WWW provides a multimedia environment that offers colorful graphics, animated screen displays, sound files, photographs, video files, and access to most of the other Internet services described previously. For most of today's Internet users the WWW is synonymous with the Internet. However, structurally it is important to realize that the WWW is a convenient way to navigate through most Internet services. The WWW is accessed through browser programs such as Netscape Communicator or Microsoft Explorer. From one of these browsers it is possible to conduct an FTP session. In this case the user would be technically "leaving" the WWW to conduct the FTP session, and then "returning" to the WWW when the downloading was completed. The user, however, might be completely unaware that (s)he has left the WWW and then returned to it.

Locations on the WWW are accessed through the special names of those locations. Those names are called Uniform Resource Locators, or URLs. (These are the familiar web addresses such as http://houghton.edu.) Each URL has essentially four parts: the *source type* (most typically http://), the *hostname* (which names the remote computer site that holds the web page), the *path* (which may be omitted or which may be several words separated by /'s), and the *filename* (which may be omitted if the URL ends in a /.) Figure 3–4 "dissects" a typical URL. The most typical source type is http, which refers to *hypertext transfer protocol.* Examples of other sources types are ftp (for *file transfer protocol)*, gopher (used for locating files on the Internet), and telnet (for terminal emulation). Learning to read the source type part of a URL can help you identify what Internet service is being used. The second piece of the URL, the hostname, helps you identify what institution's computer is being accessed. The suffixes on the hostnames tell something about the type of institution. The suffix *.edu* indicates that a school is being accessed; *.gov* indicates that a governmental computer is being accessed; *.com* indicates that a commercial business is being accessed; *.org* indicates a non-profit

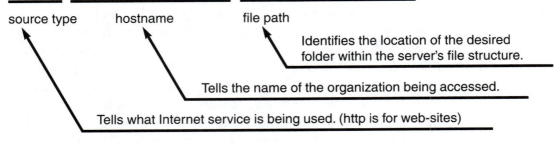

Figure 3–4.   A URL Dissected (Note: This URL has no filename at the end.)

organization. Noting the type of organization can be a helpful part of assessing the value of the information found on a given web-site. The path and the file name have little meaning for human web-users. The computer uses the path and the file name to locate the specific file that the user is requesting.

Ways to Connect

There are various ways to connect to the Internet in order to use the WWW. College students generally enjoy a *direct* connection as a result of the college or university's relationship to the Internet. Direct connections usually provide service that is quite fast, and individual users of a direct connection are not charged a subscription fee. Direct connections do not require the use of a modem or a telephone line. Many K–12 schools also enjoy the benefits of a leased-line direct connection. Teachers who expect to use the Internet in their teaching absolutely must have an Internet connection that they can access from home using a modem and a telephone line. The ideal arrangement is when the school has a direct connection that the teacher can access from home. This way the individual teacher does not have to pay a monthly access fee to a provider.

Outside of an educational institution, would-be Internet users must pay a monthly fee to a Commercial Online Service or to an Internet Service Provider. Commercial Online Services, the best-known of which is America Online, provide services in addition to their access to the Internet. (In fact, a few years ago America Online *added* Internet access to their list of services offered. Their services go far beyond the Internet services described here.) Internet Service Providers provide only that: access to the Internet. Both types of service are paid for on a monthly basis, and costs for each are roughly equivalent. Commercial Online Services provide their own software for using their services and for browsing the web. Internet Service Providers generally assume that their customers will use a browser such as Netscape Navigator or Microsoft Explorer. From the very beginning the Netscape company has made its software available free of charge for educators. There are many technical hurdles to overcome in order to connect to the Internet through an Internet Service Provider. The best advice is to ask a potential provider to provide all the necessary training and help as it is needed.

Many communities can obtain access to the Internet through a "free" connection that is available through the public library. Such connections operate under the trademark "FreeNet". Users can log on through a special account on a computer in the library, or in some cases, can dial in from home using a computer equipped with a modem.

Finding What You Want: Using Web Search Engines

One of the greatest hurdles to overcome in becoming an efficient user of the WWW is being able to filter through the vast amount of information in order to find exactly what you need. A number of Web Search Engines have been developed to help with this task. Since this is one of the difficulties in using the Internet, it is also one of the fastest changing areas. Developers are constantly improving the search engines, and it is likely that by the time you are reading this, new products will have been introduced. Therefore, rather than describing the use of a particular search engine, we highlight some general principles of how to conduct an efficient web search.

The first and most obvious task in searching the web is to locate sites that contain the information you are looking for. However, a more difficult part of a good search is to limit the parameters of your search so that you find a reasonable number of sites that contain what you need. Finding 20,000 sites that contain the word "volcanoes" will not help you use Internet resources in your teaching. So, an effective search locates appropriate sites but in a small enough number to be useful. These goals are accomplished through choosing carefully the terms that will be used in the search.

All search engines provide a form or a blank in which the user types the search terms. A single-word search term will almost always turn up more "hits" than are useful. Therefore, the beginning of a good search is to choose a phrase for the search term, or to use a combination of search terms. Search engines vary in the way they handle phrases or multiple-word search terms, but they all allow words to be combined with the AND operator. To narrow the "volcanoes" term it would be possible to search for "volcanoes AND lesson-plans" for example. The "AND" operator functions to narrow a search a great deal. Another operator that is helpful in narrowing a search is the "NOT" operator. Usually this operator is used in conjunction with AND in the following way: volcanoes AND "lesson plans" AND NOT elementary. This search will find sites that specify that there are volcano lesson plans, but it will exclude those that are designated as elementary. A third operator is usually used when the search needs to be broadened rather than narrowed. That operator is "OR". The following search will reveal sites that might have useful teaching information but which neglected to identify it as a lesson plan: volcanoes AND "lesson plans" OR resources. These three operators, which are known as Boolean operators, are used to conduct highly effective Internet searches.

The best search engines return a list of hits in which the "best" matches are at the top of the list. Therefore, even if your search turns up hundreds of hits, probably the first ten are worth examining even before you try a narrower search.

CLASSROOM USE OF THE INTERNET

As a Static Source of Information

One of the common uses that teachers make of the Internet is to find resources needed for teaching. We refer to this as a "static" use of the Internet, because it implies that the resources are sitting "out there" somewhere on the Internet and the teacher is going and retrieving them. (Note: The resources that the teacher is accessing are usually not totally static, but the fact that the resources exist for retrieval is static.) This is using the Internet in much the same way that previous generations used libraries or curriculum resource centers. The teacher needs a satellite photograph weather map for a weather lesson, and she goes to the Internet, and finds and retrieves the map for use in her lesson the next day. (This can be accomplished at http://wxweb.msu.edu/weather.)

Dynamic Interactive Uses

Interactive uses of the Internet are distinctively different from information-gathering uses. In this case the Internet is being used to bring people together in order to create a dialog. Dialog between diverse parties is an important component of constructivist learning. With interactive uses of the computer the desired outcome (knowledge) does not exist until the dialog occurs. There is not some information resource "out there" to be gathered, but rather, information arises from the dialog. We refer to such uses of the Internet as "dynamic."

Classroom-to-Classroom

One model of dynamic Internet use occurs when teachers use the Internet to enable their classrooms to collaborate on a project. An organization that promotes classroom-to-classroom projects is the International Education and Resource Network (I*EARN) http://www.iearn.org/iearn/. This organization forms "Learning Circles" of about 6 to 8 classrooms from various geographic areas for specific projects that run for about a 14-week period. The projects vary greatly, but revolve around a theme issue. (One recent theme issue was "Places and Perspectives," which was meant to examine various areas' local history, culture, government, and geography.) There is a cycle of activities that the Learning Circles follow. In the beginning the classes make an initial acquaintance and get to know who is participating, where they are from, and so on. Following this, each participating class posts a description of the project that they would like to complete. Along with this project description is a description of the involvement that will be requested from each of the other participating classes. (Typical requests for involvement might include having the participating classes complete a survey.) Over the next few weeks the participating classes respond to one another's requests for involvement. Following this, each class spends time assembling and analyzing the materials that they have received from their Learning Circle participants. The final outcome goal is for each classroom to produce a publication that summarizes the project and presents in a meaningful way the material that they have gathered. Each class shares their product with every class in the Circle.

The I*EARN organization provides much assistance to teachers who participate. A sample of some of their project guidelines is shown in Figure 3–5. This is only one organization of many that serve to provide a structure for teachers to use to bring their classrooms into contact with each other. Membership in I*EARN requires payment of a membership fee, and membership is required for participation in the Learning Circles.

CHARACTERISTICS OF SUCCESSFUL LEARNING CIRCLE PROJECTS

1. The information requested is likely to show interesting cultural and regional variation. Projects should be designed to take advantage of the diversity represented in the Learning Circle. Having students investigate the characteristics of their own environment in relationship to others is a very effective teaching and learning tool.

2. The request for project information is reasonable in scope and can be completed without a large investment of classroom time. Remember, there will be many interesting Learning Circle projects sponsored in your Learning Circle. In most cases, participating teachers should be able to organize a response to your project across one or two class periods.

3. The sponsored project extends the classroom curriculum. Learning Circle projects are an especially effective way to learn when they are tied to more extensive learning activities that take place in the classroom. Adding regional information to your lessons or providing a "hands on" cooperative learning activity to demonstrate a concept are very effective ways of extending classroom instruction.

4. The project information collected will be of interest to a wide audience of students, teachers, parents, and others who read the publication. The Circle publication summarizing the collected information is a unique and current document. The student viewpoint as well as the information itself can be of great interest to other students and adults in the community.

Figure 3–5.   "Characteristics of Successful Learning Circle Projects"
From http://www.att.com/education/lcguide/p3.plan/3.projects.html. Copyright 1996 AT&T Co.

Person-to-Person

Another form of dynamic interactive use of the Internet is person-to-person contact through e-mail. The most common type of person-to-person contact is through keypal exchanges. (The modern version of penpals.) Many organizations exist to help teachers to find suitable keypal connections for their students. One such organization that promotes international keypal exchanges is the Intercultural E-mail Classroom Connect (IECC) organization. This organization provides many services beyond simple keypal exchanges, but this is one of their services. Their web location is http://www.stolaf.edu/network/iecc/. Without some guidance from the teacher, keypal exchanges rarely progress much beyond a simple exchange of greetings and questions about interests. However, wise teachers can help their students pose questions of a nature that will enrich the curriculum. For example, classes studying ancient Greece might ask a keypal living in Greece today if (s)he has ever visited any of the ancient ruins, and what reaction (s)he had to seeing them firsthand.

Another type of person-to-person e-mail contact occurs through various ask-an-expert services. Perhaps the best known of these is Ask Dr. Math, which is available for K–12 students to have their math questions answered. Students send their math questions to dr.math@forum.swarthmore.edu. Within a short time their answer is returned via e-mail. Ask Dr. Math is operated by Swarthmore College's Steven Weimer, and the questions are answered by Swarthmore math students and professors as well as volunteer mathematicians from around the world. There are numerous ask-an-expert services available, and a listing of them can be found at http://www.askanexpert.com/askanexpert/.

Person (or Classroom)-to-the World

Sometimes students or teachers use the Internet to conduct a survey. This can be done through some of the listservs or newsgroups that are found on the Internet. One interesting project that one of the authors saw was a request for viewers to flip a coin ten times and send the results (heads/tails) to the e-mail address that was given. The fifth-grade class that posted this request was conducting a probability experiment. Their goal was to obtain massive amounts of trial data from around the world. Teachers who are interested in posting requests for information or data should try to find out the parameters of the newsgroup or list that they are considering using. It is considered bad netiquette to post a request for such information on an inappropriate list.

Problem-Solving

Sometimes teachers devise ways to use the Internet itself as a problem-environment for learning. Used in this way the learning experience is derived from using the Internet to solve a problem. A high school math teacher who uses the Internet in this way is Nils Ahbel.

After helping his students pose a problem that is of genuine interest to them, Ahbel points them in directions from which they can locate data on the Internet. They are then required to find actual data, analyze it, use it in their project, and make a presentation. The presentations are to be in electronic format (spreadsheet, geometric supposer, etc.), which Ahbel makes available as downloadable files on his web page (http://www.deerfield.edu/~ahbel/)

Problems in Using the Internet

One of the greatest weaknesses of the Internet at this point in time is that it is still relatively difficult to use. In particular, it consumes a tremendous amount of time to get to know the Internet firsthand. Much of the time spent on the Internet is time spent waiting for pages to download. This becomes particularly troublesome when there are a lot of graphic images on the pages. In some ways this is a fact of life that must be accepted in order to learn to use the Internet. However, there are some small steps that can be taken to reduce the problem of excessive time waste. If the connection to the Internet is through telephone lines, it is crucial to use the fastest modem available. (Modem speeds are constantly improving, so the fastest speed at the time of this writing will certainly not be the fastest speed at the time of your reading.) Another helpful step is to set the browser so that it doesn't automatically load images. Images are nice, but they take up tremendous amounts of time. With the browser set to *not* load images it will place icons on the screen as image-markers. If it is important to see a particular image, you can click on it and that single image will download.

When teachers desire to use the Internet in the classroom, time is of the essence. It is unacceptable to spend large amounts of precious class time waiting for web pages to download. A software product that addresses this is WebWhacker from The Forefront Group, Inc. This software allows the teacher to "whack" web pages from the Internet while she is doing her preparations for class. Then, during class, she presents those whacked pages. The appearance is that the web is being surfed, but in actuality the copies of the web pages are being viewed. There is almost no time required for these copies of web pages to load. An additional benefit of this kind of "surfing" is that the locations to which unattended children can surf are controlled.

DELTA PRINCIPLE PERSPECTIVE ON THE INTERNET

The Internet was designed to enhance communication and resource sharing, primarily among first the military and then university researchers. Today's use of the Internet is beginning to go beyond what its originators imagined. Today's use of the Internet could be characterized as being a Delta Level II use. Exploration and experimentation are underway, but most of us have not yet redefined our tasks to the point where they are Internet-dependent. Although the primary uses of the Internet are still communication and resource sharing, the numbers of people and the types of people using it have changed dramatically. Because of the wide array of types of people using the Internet, there are new uses being conceived all the time. It is only a matter of time before we see widespread Delta Level III uses of the Internet. What those uses might be we can only imagine at this point. Certainly the teachers who are involved in projects with cross-cultural classroom connections are beginning to move toward Delta Level III uses of the Internet.

HYPERMEDIA AND MULTIMEDIA

The WWW is the premier example of a type of computer environment referred to as *hypermedia*. (*Hypertext* is the word used to refer to a similar environment that includes only text.) The prefix *hyper* in hypermedia refers to the fact that the information is accessed in a non-linear fashion (Nelson, 1990). Rather than reading an information space sequentially in a pre-determined order, a user of hypertext (or hypermedia) explores the information space in his or her own order, usually based on his or her interests. In a hypermedia environment there is not necessarily a beginning point to the information, nor is there an ending point, nor is there any assurance that the "reader" will be presented with all the information that is available.

Many educational software packages use a hypermedia format to make information available to learners. Since the WWW is a well-known example of hypermedia, we have chosen this chapter to examine some features of hypermedia in general.

In a hypermedia environment the distinct packages of information are referred to as *nodes.* A node of information may include text, sound, video, and so on. Nodes are connected to one another through *links.* Links are activated through special *anchors* within the node. An anchor can be a word or phrase that is highlighted, or it can be an icon or image on the page. There are many links leading out of and into each distinct node. An overview of a segment of a hypermedia environment may be conceptualized as is shown in Figure 3–6. In this particular diagram links are shown to connect the nodes in a series. A user *could* page through in the order established by these "Next" and "Back" links (labeled N and B), but the presence of alternative paths distinguishes this as a *hyper* media environment.

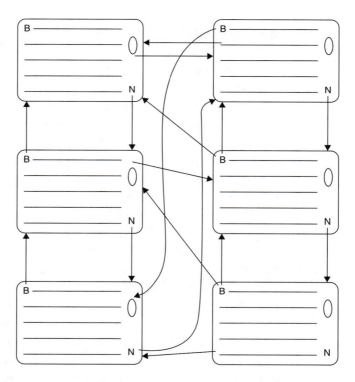

Figure 3–6.   Nodes, Links, and Anchors in a Hypermedia Environment

The use of "Next" and "Back" links in a hypermedia environment brings us to the issue of navigation in a hypermedia environment. Navigation refers to finding your way around in this type of information space, and it can be quite confusing at times. With a multitude of choices and paths to follow it is very easy for a user to become lost in a large information space. The easiest way to find your way back to familiar ground is to retrace your steps. Hypermedia environments that provide "Back" links do so in order to facilitate this backtracking. The use of "Next" links allows a user to follow a predetermined path through the information space. This feature would be useful if there were a particular order in which it was important to view the material, but it would actually defeat the purpose of using a hypermedia environment. Information that *should* be presented in a pre-determined sequence might be referred to as linear information, and it is best suited for a linear presentation medium. Books and videotapes are ideal for linear presentations.

DELTA PRINCIPLE PERSPECTIVE ON HYPERMEDIA

The use of non-linear, hypermedia environments for learning raises a number of questions. How do learners respond when they are free to roam about in a non-structured information space? Is this an efficient way to learn? How can we be sure students are learning the curriculum? Advocates of this type of learning resource argue that learners are much more motivated to learn when they can pursue their own interests. They describe such learning as more "authentic" than traditional learning in which information is presented in a pre-packaged form. To the question about efficiency, advocates of hypermedia claim that the most *in*efficient form of instruction is that which results in forgotten lessons and that which results in learning without understanding. Students who learn in a hypermedia environment, it is claimed, will remember what they learn because they are pursuing their own interests and constructing their own understandings. To the question of how we can be sure students are learning the curriculum, advocates claim that the curriculum should be broad enough to include whatever the students learn in this kind of information-rich environment. Not everyone agrees with the advocates of hypermedia learning, however. Traditional instruction has been built on the assumption that a good teacher *structures* a body of knowledge in a way that is accessible to the learner. Traditional instruction assumes that good teaching involves effective *presentation* of knowledge. These assumptions are questioned by those who advocate hypermedia learning. There is, in short, a great deal of debate surrounding hypermedia learning. What is needed is caution, a critical response to rhetoric, informed thinking, and an examination of some research findings.

Even after an examination of research on hypermedia learning, there are still questions about its effectiveness. It is important to look at the kinds of questions that the research has addressed. Are we researching the effectiveness of using a new tool to do an old job? If we are using a traditional curriculum in our research, and if our question is whether or not students and teachers with hypermedia are learning this traditional curriculum better, then perhaps we are asking the wrong questions. Since we have new tools we should be able to do new things. Our most important question is probably, "What kinds of learning experiences can we design with hypermedia that we couldn't design without it?" If we have a technology-dependent learning experience, do we really need to examine whether a technology-rich environment is more effective than a technology-poor environment?

THINK ABOUT

- Is communication via e-mail a social activity? In what ways is it inferior to face-to-face talking? In what ways is it superior? If schoolchildren spend time communicating with other people via e-mail, is the time spent on the computer time spent "in isolation"?

- The WWW has been criticized for being slow. Has it been your experience that you've had to wait great lengths of time for the web to locate certain pages or to download certain files? Are these wait-times detrimental to classroom learning? How can you make good educational use of web wait times?

- Some people have suggested that it is unwise to invest vast quantities of money into equipping classrooms for the Internet without a firm research base indicating that it improves learning. Respond to this idea. Debate it in class.

SELECTED REFERENCES

Nelson, J. (1990). *Hypertext and hypermedia.* Boston: Harcourt, Brace, Javonovich.

Rivard, J. (1997). *Quick guide to the Internet.* Boston: Allyn & Bacon.

Robichaux, J. (1996). *Frequently asked questions for schools* (No. IITA FYI 22). Internet School Networking Group.

4 Communication and Presentation Tools

LOOKING AHEAD

A few years ago an advertisement for the Xerox company pictured a monk at work busily copying a passage of the Bible by hand. When the monk saw the Xerox copier in operation he exclaimed, "It's a miracle!" The power and appeal of the advertisement came from the juxtaposition of an electronic copier with the hand-copying done by the monk. The monk, of course, symbolized an earlier technology that performed a similar function as the Xerox copier. The availability of electronic copiers has done much more than speed up our ability to duplicate written documents. In the same way, the availability of word processing and other electronic communication tools has done much more than speed up our ability to put text on paper.

According to Sheffield (1996), students in teacher education programs report higher skills in word processing than in other areas of computer use. Also, more students each year report that they have skill and experience with word processing. Because of these trends, this text does not treat beginning word processing skills in depth. Rather, the focus is on some more advanced features of word processing and on communication tools that go beyond a simple word processor.

CAN YOU?

- Describe some advanced features of word processing such as the use of formatting, outlining, tables, templates, and mail merge?

- Design a page layout that makes use of tables (columns) to optimize the effectiveness of communication?

- Give some examples of times when a teacher might use word processing templates in her daily routine?

- Describe how to place clip art in a word processing document?

- Use a set of computer drawing tools to make a simple diagram?

- Identify some sources of computer artwork?

- Tell what presentation software is used for?

- Suggest some creative uses of presentation software for teaching?

- Describe some ways that communication and presentation tools might change teachers' daily routine?

- Describe some ways that communication and presentation tools might change the way students think and learn?

TEACHER LABORATORY

Examine the teachers you have now. What evidence is there that any of them use word processing? Examine the printed materials that these teachers distribute to you in class. What evidence is there that some features of word processing helped the teacher make this document more effective? What graphic elements are included? How would you include features such as these in the document if you didn't have a word processor? Would it be worth the time and effort to do so?

Before word processing was widely available, most executives had secretaries who prepared all their documents for them. Today many executives use word processing to prepare their own documents. Some people would say that word processing has been a detriment to executives and to secretaries because of this shifting of responsibilities. See if you can find out if teachers feel the same way about the impact of word processing on *their* job responsibilities. What do you expect their answer to be? Why?

Read the following description; then look at the illustration at the end of the chapter. Compare your understanding of the material with and without the aid of the illustration. Do you achieve better understanding with the words alone? illustration alone? words and illustration together?

> High and low pressure systems are similar in that both involve rotating winds around a central area. In a high pressure system the winds rotate in a clockwise direction. In a low pressure system the rotation is counterclockwise.

WORD PROCESSING

In the 1980s the word processor replaced the typewriter as the basic tool used to put text on paper. The features and capabilities of word processors have advanced far beyond the simple functions of putting text on paper, however. Writers today need skills that include page design, font selection, the use of clip art and graphics, manipulation of white space, and even the use of video and audio to improve communication. Writers today can even insert fully functional spreadsheets into their documents. Writers can use annotations (markers which contain notes) to reflect on their writing or to leave themselves reminders as they are in the process of writing. The word processor provides a multitude of advanced tools for writers; writers must develop skills with these features in order to make effective use of them. Simultaneously, word processors have made life easier for writers through such features as the spell-check and grammar-check tools.

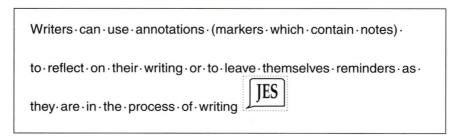

Figure 4–1.   An Annotation Marker in Some Text

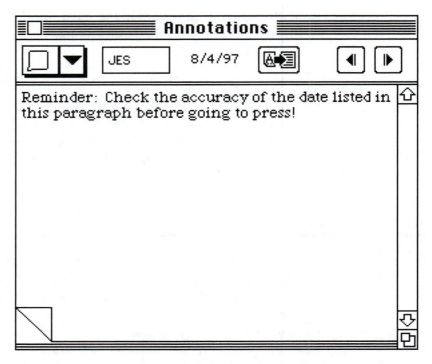

Figure 4–2.   A Sample Text Annotation (it opens after double-clicking the annotation marker)

Formatting Features

One of the first features word-processing beginners enjoy is the ability to change fonts. The use of **bold** fonts, or *italics,* or different sizes of fonts can be a way to enhance communication. These features can easily become a distraction, however, so one of the things beginners must learn is when *not* to use these features. It is very easy to create a document that has too many font changes; it is more difficult to create a document that makes effective use of these features.

Margins and tabs can also be easily controlled with word processors.* Special formats can be created to automatically indent the

---

*A note on technique: It is much wiser to use tab settings to create indentations rather than to use the space bar. If the space bar is used to create an indentation, and the writer later makes font or format changes, the spaces may change in unpredictable ways. Similarly, you should always hit return on a line above a line where there will be an indentation. If you use spaces to end a line and wrap those spaces to the next line to create an indentation, the indentation is "unstable."

first line of a paragraph, freeing the writer from the need to hit the tab key at the start of each paragraph. Other formats can be created to make hanging indents for lists. (See the Selected References lists at the end of each chapter for an example of a hanging indent.) Bulleted lists are also easily created using a word processor. If a writer is creating a numbered list, the word processor can supply the numbers after the list is written. If the writer later wants to add or subtract items from the list, the word processor can easily renumber the list.

One of the most powerful features of word processors is the ability to make a particular format combination (fonts, tabs, margins) and store it for repeated use. In Microsoft Word™ this stored format is known as a "style." The writer creates a style, gives that style a name, and saves that named style. Then, when the style is to be applied it is simply a matter of selecting that style name from a list of available styles. In this book, styles are used extensively. Each heading and subheading is a particular style. The lists in the Can You sections use another style. The Selected References lists have their own style. Even the paragraphs that contain the words you are reading are formatted in a style. The advantage to using styles is that the writer can develop a consistent set of formatting aids to communication. The reader learns what the formatting means and comes to expect clues to meaning from the formatting. Since the writer can apply these styles with a few mouse clicks it is not difficult for the writer to provide these clues to meaning.

Outlining

A word processor's outlining feature builds on and expands on the idea of styles. An outline is created using a different style for each of the different heading levels of the outline. The styles that are used for outlining are usually pre-defined by the software, but can often be modified by the user. When a writer uses the outline mode he can view the work at various levels. The writer can choose to view only the highest level headings. He can progressively open the document to show more levels of detail. Any of the headings can be double-clicked to open the details of that heading. It can then be double-clicked again to hide the details of that heading. In Figure 4–3, the plus marks to the left of the headings indicate that the document

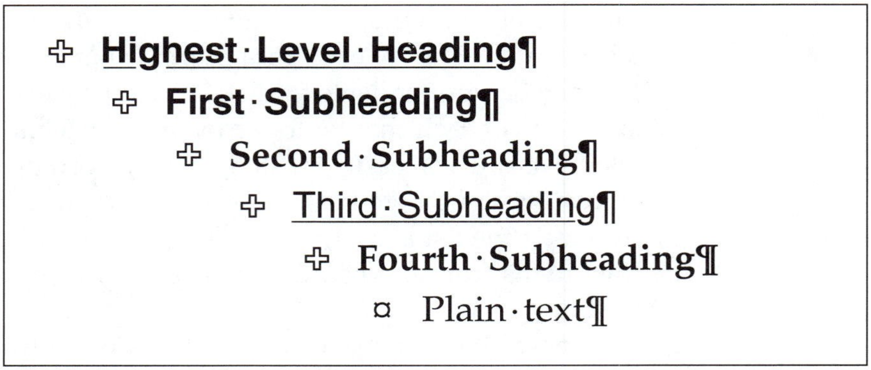

⊹ **Highest·Level·Heading¶**
  ⊹ **First·Subheading¶**
    ⊹ **Second·Subheading¶**
      ⊹ Third·Subheading¶
        ⊹ **Fourth·Subheading¶**
          ¤ Plain·text¶

Figure 4–3. **A Sample Outline in Outline View**

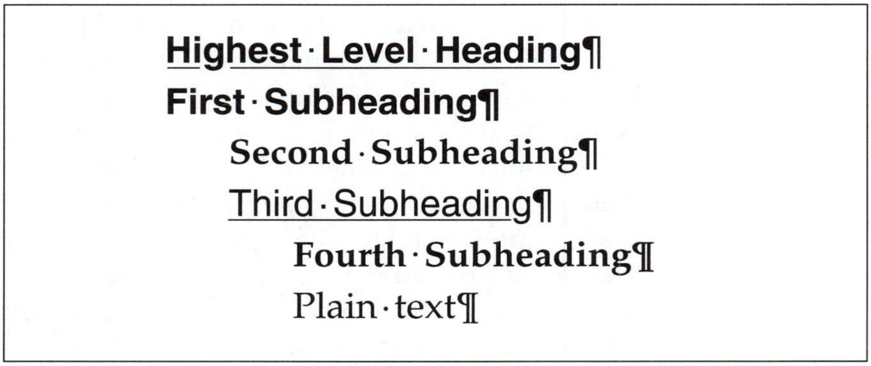

Highest·Level·Heading¶
First·Subheading¶
Second·Subheading¶
Third·Subheading¶
Fourth·Subheading¶
Plain·text¶

Figure 4–4. **The Same Outline in Normal View**

is in outline view. These plus marks are where you would double-click to open and close the text that belongs to each heading.

All of the ordinary features of word processing apply to the outline mode as well. That is, the writer can move an entire section of the outline to a different place in the document in order to experiment with the effectiveness of this type of change for improved communication. This kind of editing can be done with major heading topics or with subtopics within a major heading topic. When a topic is closed it can be dragged to a new location and all the accompanying text will move with it. Ordinarily the outlining function is used as a tool to make the writing process easier. When the document is completed it is usually not printed in outline view. When a document is printed in normal view the plus marks are not visible, and the indenting is less pronounced. However, the style formatting of the fonts remains.

Tables

When it is necessary to create columns to present information, word processors' ability to make tables is extremely helpful. A table is a row-and-column grid in which each cell can be formatted separately. (This feature is referred to as "tables" in Microsoft Word™; other word processors have different names for it.) The column width can be easily varied; adjoining cells can be merged; shading can be used to highlight cells or groups of cells; borders can be placed on any or all of the boundaries of a cell. If borders are not placed, the table itself is invisible for printing, but the text prints in crisp columns and rows. Many of the same effects could be accomplished using tabs and styles, but the flexibility afforded through tables makes learning to use them a good investment.

Templates

Word processors have the ability to store a formatted "blank" document as a template that can be used over and over again. Metaphorically, it is as if you can create a "pad of paper" with copies of specific items on each sheet of the pad. Each time you open a sheet of this "paper" you are actually opening a copy of the template. This means that the original remains unchanged regardless of how many times you use it. This is particularly useful when you need to use a form repeatedly with your students. Parts of the form, which are appropriate for every recipient of the form, can be written on the template; other parts can be filled in individually for each student. Many teachers use templates in this way to provide frequent assessment feedback to their students.

Mail Merge

Excellent teachers have always worked hard to maintain close contact with the families of the children they teach. Traditionally an occasional letter to the home was a part of this effort to keep in touch. Since the advent of word processing, it has been easier to add a more personal touch to these letters home. The mail merge feature of word processors allows the teacher to send a personally addressed letter to each parent or guardian. The names and addresses of the parents and guardians are kept on a database file, so they only need to be typed once at the beginning of the year. The letter that everyone will receive also needs to be written only once. Specially coded characters are entered into the letter to direct the word processor to fill in entries from the database file at appropriate places in the letter.

Today's word processing programs are so user-friendly that they provide step-by-step instructions for how to create a mail-merge document. For this reason we do not present such instruction in this text, but we urge readers to try out this feature on their favorite word processing program.

GRAPHICS

Clip Art

Since word processors have become the standard tool for writing, graphic objects have become more common in written materials. Few of us have the talent or the time to create our own artwork, so we use collections of graphic objects known as clip art to enhance our writing. These collections sometimes come packaged with computers or printers on disks or CDs. Other collections are commercial products in their own right. In either case, clip art objects must be assumed to be protected by copyright unless specific permission is given for free use of the clip art. In practical terms, it is usually acceptable to use clip art without gaining copyright permission in work that you will not be publishing. If you intend to publish work containing clip art, it is necessary to obtain permission from the holder of the copyright.

Inserting clip art objects into a word processing document is a simple matter. In Microsoft Word™, use the Insert menu, and select Picture. A dialog box will appear asking you to locate the graphic object that you wish to insert. ClarisWorks™ uses a similar procedure, but "Insert" from the File menu is used. In ClarisWorks™, the art can be inserted as an in-line character or as a graphic object. If it is inserted as an in-line character, the computer treats it as if it were text. It cannot be dragged around and it cannot be re-sized. It retains its position relative to the text on the page. If the text moves, the clip art moves with it. If it is inserted as a graphic object, it can be dragged around and placed anywhere on the page, it can be re-sized by clicking and dragging on its corner or sides, and text can be wrapped around it. It maintains its position on the page even though words of text may change their location on the page.

When a clip art object is placed into a word processing document, it appears in a frame that has "handles." The handles are small, black squares located in the corners and on the sides of the frame. The handles are spots that can be clicked on to drag the clip art into a new size and/or shape. The handle in the lower right corner allows you to re-size the object. If you hold the shift key down while you drag, the object is re-sized proportionally. The handles on the right side and on the bottom allow you to change the width and height of the frame.

The use of clip art can make a dramatic difference in teacher-made materials for the classroom. One area that this is often seen is in the use of maps. Clip-art maps are readily available, and teachers can use them in creating geography materials that exactly meet the needs of the children in that classroom.

Draw/Paint Applications

Although the use of clip art gives the teacher great help in creating classroom materials, there are times when it is necessary to create graphic materials "from scratch." Draw and paint applications are used to create graphic objects. Integrated software packages such as ClarisWorks™ include draw and paint applications within their suites.

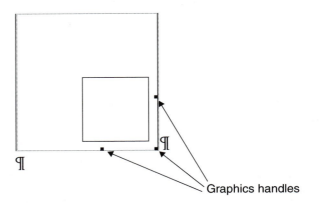

Graphics handles

Figure 4–5. A Graphics Object with Handles

("Suites" contain several different tool applications that are designed to work seamlessly together. ClarisWorks™ contains word processing, spreadsheet, database, draw, paint, and communications software.) With today's integrated software suites it is possible to create graphic objects within a word processing document. With older software the graphic object is created using the draw or paint application and it is copied and pasted into the word processing document.

Draw and paint are similar in that both are applications for creating graphics. They are different, however, in how they treat the objects that are created. Draw applications allow the user to create an *object*. For example, a polygon created in a draw environment cannot be selected, copied, moved, or edited except as a whole polygon. This is what distinguishes it as an *object*. Paint applications allow the user to create artwork by managing individual dots on the screen (which are known as pixels). A rectangle created in a paint environment is merely a series of dots that someone has put into a rectangular shape. Any of the dots can be changed without affecting the other dots. Part of a paint rectangle can be selected and moved, for example.

Draw and paint programs differ in their suitability for different types of graphics projects. Draw programs are better for projects that use a lot of defined shapes. A story web would be well-suited to a draw program. Paint programs are better suited for projects where artistic detail is important. A drawing of different types of leaves would be best suited to a paint program. The details of the different leaf shapes and edges could be much more easily accomplished using paint tools rather than draw tools. Paint tools give the artist more flexibility for creating detail. Draw tools give the artist more efficiency with graphic objects that might need to be duplicated, copied, and moved as distinct units. Draw and paint graphics are

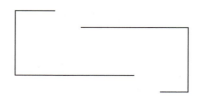

Figure 4–6.   A Rectangle Drawn in a Paint Application (it can therefore be manipulated, as shown)

also distinguished by the amount of memory it takes to store images. Images created with a paint application require a considerable amount more memory to store than do images created with a draw application.

Figure 4–7 displays the draw tool palette from ClarisWorks™ along with labels that identify the function of each of the tools. The top four tools are special. The pointer tool is used to select, resize, and move objects. ClarisWorks™ automatically reverts back to this tool after using any other tool, unless you double-click on the other tool before using it. The spreadsheet tool, the text tool, and the paint tool all allow you to insert special "frames" into the document. A spreadsheet frame in a draw document allows you to put a fully functional spreadsheet inside the draw document. A text frame in a draw document allows you to have a fully functional

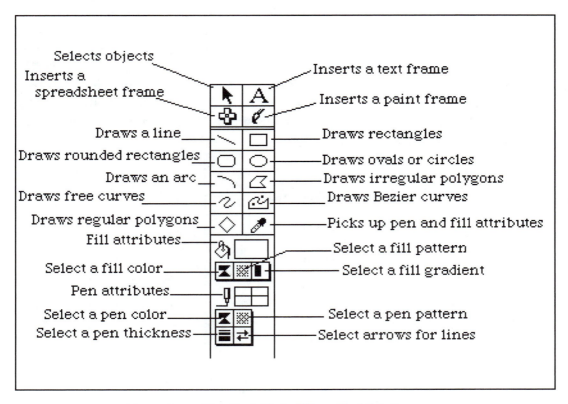

Figure 4–7.   The ClarisWorks™ Draw Tool Palette

word processing document inside the draw document. A paint frame in a draw document allows you to have a fully functional paint document within a draw document. This ability to place frames within documents extends to all the different ClarisWorks™ documents. For example, you can place a draw frame within a word processing document.

The tools that are used for drawing are somewhat self-explanatory. Many tools have this in common: when they are used with the shift key depressed their functions are constrained. With the rectangle tool, for example, the tool draws only squares when the shift key is depressed. So many applications follow this design feature that it is a good idea with any draw software to experiment with tools with the shift key depressed to see if they behave with constraints.

The paint tools in ClarisWorks™ include all of the tools used for drawing, plus some additional tools. See Figure 4–8 for the special paint tools in ClarisWorks™. The two selection tools have a similar function, but they are specially adapted to two different kinds of selection. The selection rectangle is best for selecting entire screens of graphics or isolated graphic objects on a screen. The lasso is best for selecting parts of a graphic design or irregularly shaped objects. The rectangle selection tool must be positioned above or below the object to be selected; it must also be located to the right or to the left of the object to be selected. Then it is simply dragged across the object until

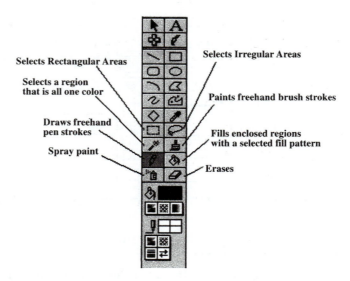

Figure 4–8. Special Paint Tools in ClarisWorks™

the rectangle surrounds the object. The lasso must encircle the object to be selected. When an object is selected with the lasso tool, its edges show the "dancing ants" phenomenon that indicate selection.

The paint bucket is an unusual tool. It is used to fill an enclosed space with "paint." The tip of the paint pouring from the bucket is the active part of this tool. Move this part of the tool into an enclosed area and click the mouse; paint will fill the area. Note: If even one pixel keeps the area from being completely closed the paint will flow out into larger areas of the screen than you want. Even the entire screen may fill with paint. If this happens you can immediately recover by using the UNDO feature in the edit menu.

The paint attributes are determined by the three palettes under the paint bucket on the toolbar. These are tear-off palettes, which means that you can drag them to another part of the screen in order to keep them open without holding the mouse down. The fill attributes that are selected with these palettes are also used by the pencil tool and the spray can. The pen attributes are determined by the tear-off palettes found beneath the pen. These attributes apply to the lines drawn by any of the draw tools.

Other Sources of Graphics

Clip-art collections and user-created graphics are not the only sources for graphics. Scanners, digital cameras, and the World Wide Web are three other important sources of graphics. All three have this in common: they all provide files of digitized images. Once these digitized image files are available, they can be placed in all kinds of documents in order to enhance communication.

Scanners

The basic function of a scanner is to turn a visual object into a form that can be read by a computer, a process known as "digitizing" the image. The visual object is usually a paper copy, but it doesn't need to be. Award plaques can be scanned as effectively as photographs can. The object to be scanned should be flat enough to fit onto the glass bed of the scanner, which is much like the bed of a photocopy machine. The software that is used in conjunction with the scanner determines the file format of the digitized image. The scanner software is also used to edit the image before storing it in digital form. Once an object or picture has been scanned and stored in digital format it is available for use in various kinds of documents. It is necessary to store the image in a format that the available word processor or draw program can read. If the image is stored in a format that is not readable, then conversion software must be used to change the format to a form that is readable.

Digital Cameras

Another source of images is the digital camera. A digital camera is much like a 35mm camera in appearance and size. However, rather than storing images on photographic film, it stores images on a miniature computer diskette. The images are then transferred directly to the computer for use in documents. The images are available immediately since there is no need for them to be sent to a developer. Software allows the user to edit the photographs. Images can be re-sized, cropped, and even "touched up" before they are used in a document. Today's color printers can even provide photographic-quality paper copies of images generated in this way.

The World Wide Web

The World Wide Web is an image-rich environment. With the web browsers that are popular today, images on the web can be captured and downloaded with a few clicks of the mouse. There are also collections of public domain and shareware graphics files available on the web. A good site to begin looking for graphics is http://members.aol.com/CapnBlue/art.html. Two popular formats for images on the web are JPEG and GIF. Newest versions of word processing and image processing software can read these file formats; older software requires format conversion software to change the file format into a readable format. With most images gathered from the web, there are copyright issues. Someone owns the copyright to all of these images, and unless permission is expressly given to copy and use them, permission must be obtained before using them.

SLIDE SHOW AND PRESENTATION SOFTWARE

Computers and projectors are now being used in tandem to create impressive large-screen presentations. The software used to create such presentations can be as simple as a feature of an integrated software package (ClarisWorks™, for example) or as sophisticated as a full-featured dedicated application (Microsoft PowerPoint™, for example). The projection devices can be LCD panels that make use of an existing overhead projector, or they can be LCD projectors that connect directly to the computer. In its simplest form an electronic slide show can consist of pages of text written in the ClarisWorks™ word processing application and presented as a slide show. In its most sophisticated form an electronic presentation can include animation, video, audio, and visits to World Wide Web home pages.

One of the advantages of using a dedicated presentation software application is that such applications provide features that help in visual design. Today's computers can produce millions of colors and virtually countless combinations of text and background colors. Microsoft PowerPoint™ provides pre-selected combinations of text and background colors that are designed to work well together. Also, such applications provide a number of background templates that are designed to provide a pleasing visual effect as the background for the slides.

Teachers can use slide show or presentation software in creative ways. The use of animation in a presentation can be used to make abstract concepts concrete. The use of color to illustrate parts of systems can be effective for helping students analyze those systems. The fact that audio and video materials can be included in presentations means that teachers can include snippets of the most effective segments of audio and video programs in their presentations. Often a two- to three-minute segment of video inserted into a teacher-made presentation is more effective than a whole video program. Furthermore, teachers can print out miniature copies of the slides and distribute them to students to enhance note-taking.

Slide shows and presentation software can be used in settings other than large-group settings. Since the pacing of the presentation can be determined by the person viewing the presentation, a slide show is ideal for a learning-center presentation for individual learning. A student viewing a slide show in an individualized setting can go forward or back or spend as long or as short a time on each slide as necessary.

Although a presentation made with a computer can be a powerful tool for communication, *any* presentation is limited in its effectiveness for helping students construct meaningful new concepts. The process of knowledge-construction is more active than passive, and viewing a presentation is primarily a passive behavior. Constructivist teachers should not dismiss presentation software as having no relevance, however. Rather than using presentation software to *make* presentations, constructivist teachers can teach their *students* to use the software to make their own presentations. A multimedia slide show, designed and produced by a team of students, can be a wonderful culminating experience for a project-oriented learning experience. With today's software this is a realistic expectation for students from the age of about grade four and up. Younger students can design simpler slide shows using the draw features of ClarisWorks™ or Kidpix™.

Another issue related to presentation software is the issue of linearity. Presentations are designed with a sequence in mind. Viewers are limited in their ability to easily explore the presentation in a different order. In contrast to this, hypermedia, such as is found on the World Wide Web, allows viewers to explore in a non-linear fashion. In a hypermedia environment, links allow spontaneous exploration of information according to the interests of the learner rather than according to the structured plan of the presenter. When the goal is to introduce a learner into an information-rich environment in order to stimulate problem-posing and pursuit of individual interests, a hypermedia environment is probably preferable to a presentation. On the other hand, when what is desired is an expert mind guiding a novice into unfamiliar territory, a presentation is probably the best method.

DELTA PRINCIPLE PERSPECTIVE

In order to apply the Delta Principle to these communication and presentation tools it may be helpful to consider the following questions:

- How might these tools change the way teachers manage their daily routine?

- How might these tools change the way learners obtain, process, evaluate, and produce knowledge?

Management of the Daily Routine

Clearly the word processor has already replaced the typewriter as the tool of choice for written communication. Word processors make editing and revision easier, and more likely. They make the job of spelling correctly easier by providing suggestions about possible misspelled words. They make creation of some documents easier by permitting re-use of portions of text. All of these benefits come from the use of basic word processing features. How might the use of formatting features and outlining capabilities, the use of tables, templates, and mail merge change the way teachers manage their daily routine?

One possibility is that these communication tools will help teachers become more dependent on instructional materials that they produce themselves than on materials that they purchase. Major curriculum materials such as course textbooks and curriculum guides will still probably come from professional sources. But materials to supplement the curriculum will perhaps come from the teachers themselves rather than from the inexpensive booklets of reproducible materials that are so readily available. The benefit to this change would be that the quality of the materials will be better. The materials that a teacher makes herself will have direct application to her students and to her curriculum. The fit between the curriculum and the supplementary materials will be excellent.

Another way in which word processors can improve teaching materials is through the use of the outlining capabilities of word processors. If teachers use outlining to create their lesson plans they will be able to easily modify those lesson plans after teaching them the first time. Major points in the lesson can be written as major outline points. The lesson plan can be viewed from the perspective of its major points. These points can be re-arranged and re-ordered as the teacher reflects on the effectiveness of the lesson as originally written. Since the outlining feature of word processing invites such editing, it is more likely that teachers will become dependent on this feature as they plan and revise their lessons. The resulting improvement and evolution of the lessons will be of benefit to students.

Another possibility is that these tools will result in more frequent communication between the teachers and the parents. The use of mail merge makes it easy enough to write letters home that teachers might develop habits of regular and frequent letters to parents. Such communication can contribute to a better sense of teamwork in helping students learn.

Student Learning

Can word processing, computer graphics, and presentation software change the way learners obtain, process, evaluate, and produce knowledge? Primarily these tools will affect how children learn written forms of communication. As such, the question is treated in depth in chapter 9. However, we can answer the question in a general way here. The greatest potential of these tools is their potential to influence the way children define written communication.

Where a former generation was concerned about putting words on paper as the primary form of communication, children preparing to enter the twenty-first century will depend on visual design as part of their concept of written communication. Virtually all formal communication today has a visual design element. Text-based communication includes page design, including the use of columns, chunking of text, headings and subheadings, borders and lines, white-space management, and purposeful selection and placement of graphics. Today all writers can employ techniques of page design to help them get their message across. In time, writers will become so accustomed to using these techniques that they will become dependent on them and will be hampered in their ability to communicate their meanings without them. One can imagine that as visual design becomes more important, the *number* of words needed to communicate an idea may be reduced. Therefore, children learning to write with today's technological tools will view the act of writing as a text-visual task. Their use of graphics will exceed that of former generations, and they may use fewer words to communicate than did former generations.

Presentation software has the potential to affect children's learning in two distinct ways. One effect will come from receiving an increasing proportion of their lessons from teachers using presentation software. The other effect will come from having to produce electronic presentations of their own.

The first effect, the effect of receiving information in the form of teacher-created electronic presentations, is actually a part of a larger issue. More and more of the information children receive is coming to them in the form of visual information. Children gain less information by reading, by listening, and by direct experience than was the case a generation ago. Children's "listening" skills have grown to include listening and watching. At the same time their attention span has been influenced by television programming. In order to gain children's attention in an environment where visual stimulation is abundant, teachers must use a visual medium. Children have already become dependent on a technologically induced visual learning environment, and presentation software helps teachers meet their needs. So one effect of presentation software on children's learning is that it more easily engages their attention than do other forms of presentation.

When children themselves are the authors of the electronic presentations there are important changes that can take place in how they think. The act of creating a slide show involves defining and composing screen-sized chunks of information. Children learning to make such presentations will, over time, become natural at thinking of their message in screen-sized chunks. The unit of one screen can only contain a limited amount of information. The transition from one screen to another must be smooth and conceptually appropriate. The placement of words and graphic elements on a screen must be done so as to carry meaning. Elements that repeat on a series of screens or on all screens of a presentation must be planned.

Some concepts, thoughts, arguments, and chains of reasoning do not lend themselves to presentations in screen-sized chunks. If teachers do not help their students to decide when an electronic presentation is *inappropriate*, then some kinds of complex thinking will be inappropriately reduced to screen-sized chunks. Communicators who can make decisions about the most appropriate technology to use to communicate a particular idea will be more powerful communicators than those who use one technology for every message.

Since these tools for communication and presentation are so new we have really only begun to imagine how they might effect the learning and thinking of students. What seems clear is that as the use of these tools becomes pervasive in our educational environments, we need to be observant and perceptive to note the changes as they occur. We need to be able to encourage changes that are beneficial and mitigate changes that are harmful. By becoming aware of the potential power of these tools, we put ourselves in a position to direct the changes that occur.

THINK ABOUT

- How might your life change if we had to go back to using typewriters for all our written communication?

- The chalkboard has been a powerful tool for teachers for a long time. Teachers often make diagrams and sketches on the chalkboard to help students "see" a concept. Will the use of computer graphics be more or less time-consuming for teachers than drawing on the chalkboard? Discuss this with your peers; try to uncover all the implications of the question.

- We made the claim that children in today's world need more visual stimulation in school because the culture is permeated with visual stimulation. Do you agree or disagree with this claim? Argue both sides in class.

- If the use of these tools becomes more of a time-consumer than a time-saver for teachers, should teachers stop using these tools? Debate the issue.

- Have you attended a presentation that was made using Power-Point or a similar computer presentation software? Was it more or less effective in communicating than the presentation would have been without the help of the computer? What aspects of the presentation were most enhanced by the computer? What aspects of communication suffered as a result of the computer?

- At the writing of this text the cost of an overhead projector and an LCD panel to project a computer image is under $2000. The cost of an LCD projector to display a computer image is at least $5000. The LCD panel and overhead require a completely darkened room, and the image produced is dim and hard to read. The image from an LCD projector is clear even in a dimly lighted room. If a school is having difficulties finding money to replace an old and failing furnace, what should they do about getting equipment for computer presentations?

• It takes a tremendous amount of time for a teacher to put together an excellent instructional presentation with animation, sound, and video. Although the resulting product is better than any commercial product because of its exact fit to the teacher's curriculum, there is a problem with stretching a teacher's time too thin. What creative ideas do you have for how to solve this problem?

SELECTED REFERENCES

Sheffield, C. J. (1996). "An examination of self-reported computer literacy skills of preservice teachers." *Action in Teacher Education,* 17(4), 45–52.

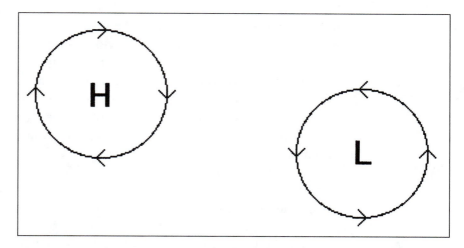

Figure 4–9. **Illustration for "Teacher Laboratory" (prepared with simple "drawing" tools)**

5 Computation and Information Tools

LOOKING AHEAD

Jamar, a first-year teacher, was standing in line in the post office. Behind him in the line he overheard two women talking about the teachers in the community. "I can't believe they're going to give those teachers a 3 percent raise again! Do you realize how easy they've got it? They only have to work from 8:00 to 3:00, they have summers off, and they get about four weeks off during the year! That would be like having a part-time job! What do they do to deserve a raise?"

Jamar had to use strong self-control to keep from turning around and setting these people straight. He knew that he was working seven days a week and that most of his days began at 7:00 AM and ended in exhaustion at about 10:30 PM. He knew about the mountain of paperwork that was piled up on his desk at home. He knew about the record-keeping, the grading, the lesson planning, the preparations, the phone calls and letters to parents, and so on that consumed all his waking hours. He also knew that this was not the time or place to try to "educate" these people about what the job of teaching really involved. Instead of trying to change them, Jamar began to wonder if there were ways that he could make parts of his job easier without cutting corners. Were there any ways he could use technology to do some of the things he had to do?

CAN YOU?

- Describe what a spreadsheet is and how it can help a teacher manage her responsibilities?

- Describe some benefits to keeping a gradebook on a spreadsheet?

- Compose some "what-if" questions that you could explore if your gradebook were kept on a spreadsheet?

- Identify some tasks that you could perform using a spreadsheet integrated with a word processing document?

- Describe what an electronic database is and how such a tool can help a teacher manage his responsibilities?

- Design a sample database that might be used for keeping student records?

- Identify some tasks that you could perform using a database and word processor together?

- Identify some ways that your management of teaching might be improved through the use of spreadsheets and databases?

TEACHER LABORATORY

Using your instructor's choice of software, construct a spreadsheet that could be used as a gradebook. Include formulas for determining students' averages. Try to find a way to give different weight to daily assignments and to tests.

Using your instructor's choice of software, construct a database that could be used for keeping important records on students. What are the specific pieces of information that you think should be included about each student?

A NOTE

The focus of this chapter is on two versatile tool applications: spreadsheets and databases. The goal here is to introduce these tools to the reader and to identify some ways these tools can help the teacher in daily management tasks. Our belief is that if the teacher becomes comfortable with (and dependent on?) these tools for her own management, then she will be able to find creative ways to use these tools to help children learn. Later chapters deal specifically with how these tools can be used to help children learn.

SPREADSHEETS

What Are Spreadsheets?

Spreadsheets are one of the most versatile computer applications in use today. Historically speaking, the development of the earliest computer spreadsheet was a major factor in the early popularity of personal computers in the business place. Prior to the invention of the spreadsheet, computer users had to write custom software for their particular "number-crunching" tasks. The spreadsheet is a general-purpose calculation application that can be used, without special programming knowledge, in almost any setting. This general-purpose design, combined with the fact that business people could computerize their office calculations without having to hire their own programmers, meant that the benefits of computers could justify their costs.

A spreadsheet is, in appearance, a grid in which the columns are labeled with letters and the rows are labeled with numbers. Figure 5–1 shows the upper left corner of a simple, blank spreadsheet. Each box where a column and row meet is known as a cell, and each cell has its own distinct letter-number address. Cell A1 is the cell at the top left corner. In Figure 5–1, cell A1 is highlighted, and the address of the highlighted cell shows in the band across the top of the spreadsheet. Numbers and formulas can be entered into the cells. Formulas can operate on the numbers found in other cells. Text can also be entered into the cells making it easy to label rows and columns. The width of the columns can easily be adjusted by clicking and dragging them to be wider or narrower. In the same way, the height of the rows can be adjusted by clicking and dragging them to be taller or shorter.

Some people use blank spreadsheets to make tables in their word processing documents. In integrated software packages a spreadsheet can be inserted directly into a word processing document. It can be used as a fully functional spreadsheet, or it can be used simply as a convenient way to create columns and rows for text. The borders of any or all of the cells can be outlined with various thicknesses of lines, allowing the writer to create a variety of formats for charts.

Ploger, et al. (1997) describe a simple example of using a spreadsheet to generate a list of even numbers. The user enters a starting number (2) into cell A1. Then in cell A2 a formula is entered: =A1+2. This formula instructs the computer to take the contents of cell A1 and add 2 to that. The result of this calculation will be displayed in

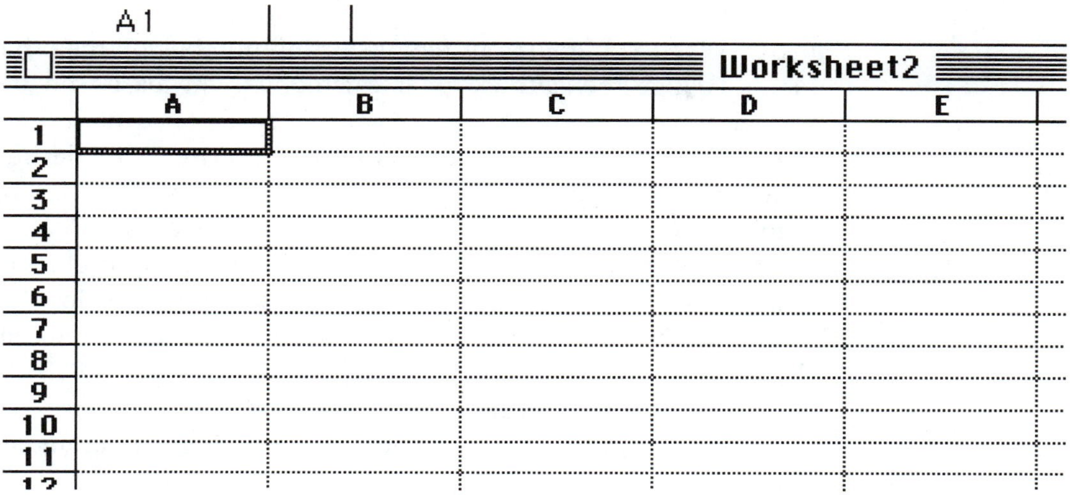

A1

	A	B	C	D	E
1					
2					
3					
4					
5					
6					
7					
8					
9					
10					
11					
12					

Worksheet2

Figure 5–1.   A Simple Spreadsheet

cell A2. By clicking and dragging from A2 to A10, and then selecting
Fill Down from the Edit menu, you can place a version of this formula in each cell between A3 and A10. The computer will modify
the formula so that it is appropriate to the row it is in. The formula in
A3 will be =A2+2, the formula in A4 will be =A3+2, and so on. The
appearance of a spreadsheet set up like this is shown in Figure 5–2.

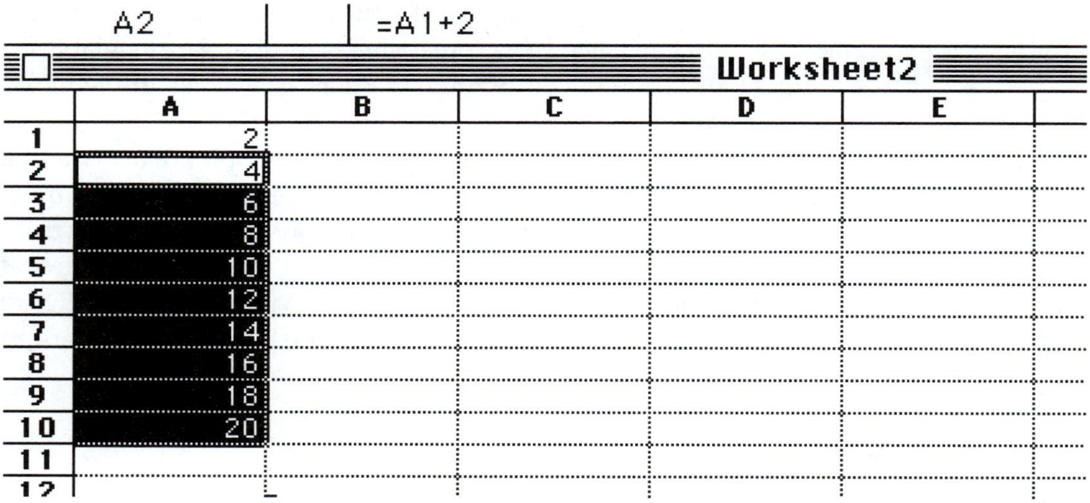

A2   =A1+2

	A	B	C	D	E
1	2				
2	4				
3	6				
4	8				
5	10				
6	12				
7	14				
8	16				
9	18				
10	20				
11					
12					

Worksheet2

Figure 5–2.   Even Numbers on a Spreadsheet

The starting number, 2, which is found in cell A1, can be changed. When you enter a different starting number, all the other numbers change too because their calculations are based on the starting number. It is this feature of spreadsheets that has made them so popular. Once a spreadsheet is set up to perform all the desired calculations for a specific problem, the input numbers can be changed in order to explore the effects of those changes. Exploration of "what-if" questions becomes a viable way of solving problems. With a spreadsheet that analyzes loans, a consumer can explore the effects of varying interest rates on the total cost of the loan. Alternatively, she can explore the effects of varying pay-back periods. With a spreadsheet that records and computes students' grades, a teacher can explore what grades a student needs on remaining assignments in order for that student to pass a course.

When you look at the spreadsheet on the computer screen you see the numbers that result from the calculations. It is only when you click on an individual cell that you see the formula that is stored in that cell. When you do click on an individual cell, the formula appears in the band across the top of the spreadsheet. This band is also where you edit any formulas.

A spreadsheet that contains formulas, as this one does, might be usable by many different people without modification. Other users would supply their own data (numbers), but the function of the spreadsheet on that data would be the same. Spreadsheets that are designed to provide specific sets of mathematical formulas for specific tasks are called *templates*. Spreadsheet templates are available for a number of specific, complex tasks such as teacher gradebooks, mortgage amortization schedules, and so on.

One of the especially powerful features of spreadsheets is the ease with which they can present data in graphic form. In most cases the data that you want to present in graphic form simply need to be highlighted and then copied and pasted into a *chart*. Then you make a selection from a menu of different types of graphs. Figure 5–3 shows the data worksheet and a spreadsheet-generated graph of one class's pizza sales over a 5-month period.

How Can Spreadsheets Help Teachers?

Probably the most potent use of a spreadsheet for teachers is as a gradebook. Although there are commercial software gradebook ap-

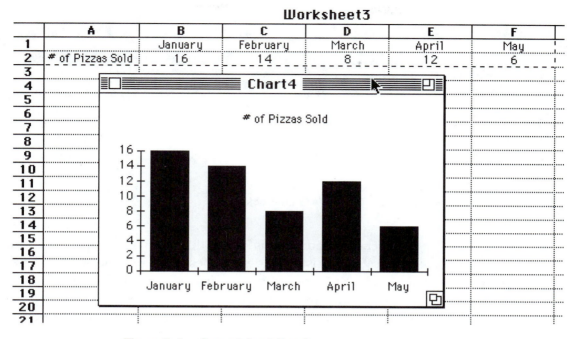

Figure 5–3.   Spreadsheet Graph

plications available, the spreadsheet can be used for all the functions of a gradebook without the need for an additional software purchase. Special gradebook application software often forces the teacher to fit the design of the program. With a little knowledge of spreadsheets, a teacher can set up a gradebook spreadsheet that does exactly what he needs.

A teacher setting up a spreadsheet gradebook would begin by assigning one row of the spreadsheet to each student. Student names would be entered into column A. Then each subsequent column of the spreadsheet would be used for grades for specific assignments. Column B might be grades on a quiz, column C might be grades on a test, column D could be used for anecdotal comments, and so on. A spreadsheet created in this manner would look like the one shown in Figure 5–4. Each new item that the teacher grades can be entered into a column of the spreadsheet. A column further to the right could be used for whatever calculation the teacher wanted to perform to determine an overall grade. If the calculation desired was an average, the formula =AVERAGE(B2:B10) might be used to compute an average of all the numbers in cells B2 through B10.

A1			Student Name	

Teacher Gradebook

	A	B	C	D
1	Student Name	Quiz #1	Midterm Exam	Anecdotal Records
2	Anthony, Susan	87	89	Argues strongly about fairness issues (2/14)
3	Douglass, Frederick	78	90	Showing good growth in speaking abilities (3/8)
4	Gates, Bill	60	72	Has a hard time concentrating on school work (1/18, 2/3)
5	Walters, Barbara	99	92	Great job on her book report (3/10)
6				
7				
8				
9				
10				

Figure 5–4.   Teacher's Gradebook

If a teacher's gradebook is kept in this way it is a simple matter to make a copy of the list of student names, paste this copy into a blank spreadsheet, and print out a class list with columns of checkboxes next to each student's name. Such class lists serve innumerable purposes for teachers. They can be used for everything from attendance lists to checklists for field trip permission forms turned in.

When teachers organize fund-raising events for their classes, there are important financial records that must be kept. The spreadsheet is an ideal tool for keeping track of these financial records. In a typical fund-raising event, each child in the class is given responsibility to sell as many items (magazine subscriptions for example) as possible. Again, the class list could be copied from the gradebook and pasted into a new spreadsheet. Columns could be used to record daily or weekly sales amounts. A column could be used to compute a total sales figure for each child. A row below the last student in the class could be used for computation of the daily sales total. A grand total could be computed by using a cell to compute the sum of all the daily totals. This figure could be compared to a grand total of the sum of all the student totals. If these totals and grand totals formulas are in place from the very beginning of the sale, any discrepancies or missing money can be spotted immediately when the books are checked daily. An example of this type of fund-raising spreadsheet is shown in Figure 5–5. In Figure 5–5, cell E8 is highlighted. This illustrates the formula, =SUM(B8:D8), which is in cell E8. The formula appears in the formula band at the top, but the result of the computation ($409.50) appears in the cell.

| E8 | | | =SUM(B8:D8) | | |

Fund Raiser

	A	B	C	D	E	F
1	Student Name	Day 1 Sales	Day 2 Sales	Day 3 Sales	Total Sales (Child)	
2	Anthony, Susan	$16.00	$5.00		$21.00	
3	Douglass, Frederick	$13.50	$15.00		$28.50	
4	Gates, Bill	$113.00	$209.00		$322.00	
5	Walters, Barbara	$25.00	$13.00		$38.00	
6						
7					$409.50	Child Total
8	Total Sales (Daily)	$167.50	$242.00	$0.00	$409.50	Daily Total
9						

Figure 5–5. Fund-Raising Spreadsheet

DELTA PRINCIPLE PERSPECTIVE ON SPREADSHEETS

When teachers use spreadsheets to help manage their responsibilities, how does this change the way they do their job? What are the Delta Principle changes that occur?

Spreadsheets as gradebooks offer a number of unique advantages over paper and pencil gradebooks. There are also some unique dangers associated with spreadsheets as gradebooks. One of the obvious advantages is the time savings for the teacher when it comes time to determine grades. Before spreadsheets were available teachers needed to manually compute each student's grade. Once the grades and the formulas are entered into a spreadsheet it takes virtually no time to compute grades. The time saved on doing manual computations is time that is available for tasks more directly related to pedagogy. This time savings might be considered a Level I benefit of using spreadsheets for gradebooks.

A more powerful benefit is the advantage that comes from being able to answer students' "what-if" questions concerning their grades. The following vignette illustrates this benefit in-action.

Earlier in the unit Shawn had missed a lot of school and his grades in algebra had dropped. Now, with the midterm approaching, Shawn had come to Mrs. Reed to talk about his grades.

Shawn: Mrs. Reed, can you tell me how I'm doing in algebra? I know my grade is low, but I don't know how low.

Mrs. Reed: Let's take a look at my gradebook. Well, right now, if the quarter were to end, your average would be 56%. Your absences have really hurt you. I see you've shown some improvement since you came in last week for extra help. Let's suppose you get 100% on the midterm. What would that do to your average? A 100% on the midterm would raise your average to a 63%.

Shawn: I probably can't get 100%, Mrs. Reed. I've never gotten 100% on a math test.

Mrs. Reed: What do you reasonably think you might earn on the midterm?

Shawn: What if I got a 90%?

Mrs. Reed: If you got a 90% your average now would be 61%.

Shawn: 61% is better than 56%, but it still isn't passing. Will I be able to pass this quarter, Mrs. Reed?

Mrs. Reed: I don't see why not. Let's see what happens if I put in 90s for all the rest of your grades. That would bring your average up to 75%. That's passing; do you think you can average 90s for the rest of the quarter.

Shawn: I don't know, but if it will turn my grade into a 75% I'll sure try.

There are many benefits to the student in the preceding vignette. When a student can receive the kind of feedback on his performance that Mrs. Reed gave Shawn, he can see directly the connection between his daily efforts and his grades. Instead of waiting until the end of the quarter to find out how they're doing, students can find out at any point during the quarter. This can have a motivating effect on students, as shown in the vignette. Another benefit Shawn received was the benefit of being asked to assess his own performance. Was it likely that he'd get 100% on the midterm? Instead of telling Shawn what his potential was or wasn't, Mrs. Reed asked Shawn for his own assessment. Not all of these benefits are directly attributable to the fact that Mrs. Reed kept her gradebook on a spreadsheet. However, the ease with which she could perform these "what-if" analyses made it much more likely that she would take the time to do so. It is almost inconceivable that a teacher might take the time to do what Mrs. Reed did if her gradebook were kept in a pencil-and-paper format. This use of the spreadsheet represents a Delta Level III benefit of the computer.

One of the unique dangers associated with keeping grades on a spreadsheet is the potential for students to gain unauthorized access to the gradebook and change their grades. With a pencil and paper gradebook it is highly unlikely that a student would ever succeed in attempting to change his grades. However, when grades are stored on computers there is a danger that such unauthorized access will occur, especially when dealing with older students. In most cases if such unauthorized access did occur it would be very difficult to detect. Teachers who use electronic gradebooks must take special precautions to prevent unauthorized access. They must not leave the computer unattended in an unlocked classroom. They must use protection software that requires a password for access to the computer and to the gradebook. If their computers are attached to networks and/or to the Internet, they need to get assurances from their network administrators that proper security is in place to prevent access from outside. If it is at all possible, it is best to use computers that are not networked for storing and processing grades.

Another unique danger associated with electronic gradebooks is the potential for losing data. If a teacher keeps her grades on a single hard disk drive and that hard disk drive fails, all of the grades will be lost and probably be unrecoverable. This would obviously be a disaster. Teachers need to plan for this event by keeping backup copies of all their gradebooks. There are a variety of ways to do this, but the important aspect is the daily discipline of actually performing the backup. With a current backup copy available, a teacher's gradebook is protected in the event of an equipment failure. If a backup copy is not current, it is of little value.

DATABASES

What Are Databases?

Another extremely versatile computer application is database software. Database software is designed to allow the user to easily record, organize, store, sort, and analyze all kinds of data. As with spreadsheets, database software is general-purpose software, and the user does not need any programming ability in order to use it. Database software is used in situations where there are numerous distinct units of information (such as students in a class) and each of these units has its own particular data (such as address, parents' names, phone number, and so on). Libraries use database software to catalog their collections. Employers use database software to keep standard information about their employees. Sociologists develop databases to catalog information about our culture. Merchants use databases to keep track of their inventories.

A database is composed of individual *records,* or units of information. Each record has its data organized into *fields.* In a representation of a database, Figure 5–6 illustrates records and fields in a database that a fisherman might keep on his catches. In this illustration all of the information on one fish caught constitutes one record, and the individual bits of information about each fish (type, where caught, lure or bait used, sky conditions, wind, and temperature) constitute the fields. Further, the specific data (Lake Trout, off Smith's Point, minnow, sunny, calm, 78°) constitute *entries* into the various fields. Part of the power of electronic databases is their ability to present the data in various formats. One could view the information on each individual record, as presented in figure 5–6. Alternatively, one could look at all the entries for specified fields for the entire database. For example, as shown in Figure 5–7, a list could be generated showing all the fish and their weights.

Another major reason why databases are so popular is the way they enable the user to search for specific data. In a small database such as the fisherman's example, it is not necessary to have the power of a computer to search for specific information. But when the volume of data in a database is large, it is vital to use computing power to search for needed information. Some teachers have databases of information that their students have been collecting for many years. (One class collects information about inventors each year, and the students in the class add the information they find to the database that has been used in this way for several years.) In such cases there may be thousands of records and tens of thousands of data entries. An example might be a database composed of members of students' family trees. A single family tree might contain 20 or more ancestors. If students have been entering data on their family trees for a few years, there can be thousands of records. If a student wanted

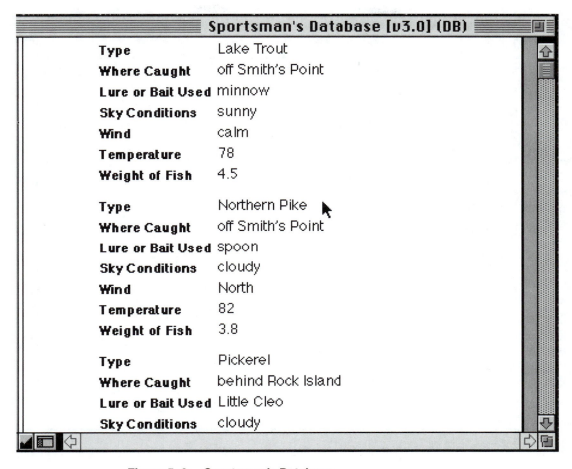

Figure 5–6.   Sportsman's Database

to search that database to generate a list of all the people who were alive during the Civil War, that would be a search that would require computing power. In today's "Information Age" the skill of using electronic databases to search for needed information is vital. Those who have developed this skill have a distinct advantage over those who have not.

In addition to electronic searching, databases can be used to quickly sort the records using any of a number of criteria. Records can be alphabetized for ease of visual or manual searching. Alternatively, records can be placed in numerical order using numerical data from one of the fields as the sort key. Complex sorts can be done in which the entire database is arranged in alphabetical order and the records are sorted numerically within each letter grouping

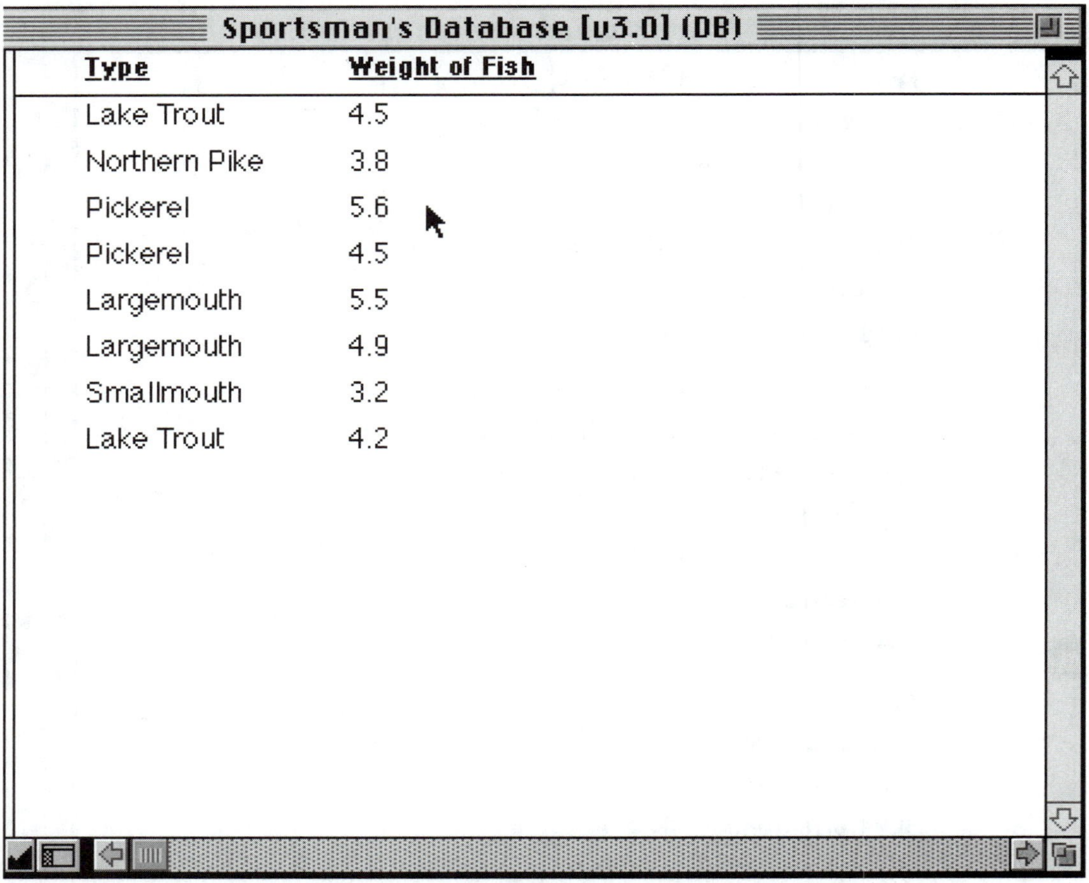

```
═══════════════ Sportsman's Database [v3.0] (DB) ═══════════════ ▣▤
  Type              Weight of Fish                                    ⇧
  Lake Trout            4.5
  Northern Pike         3.8
  Pickerel              5.6  ▶
  Pickerel              4.5
  Largemouth            5.5
  Largemouth            4.9
  Smallmouth            3.2
  Lake Trout            4.2


                                                                     ⇩
◪▢ ⇦▥          ⇨▣
```

Figure 5–7.   Sportsman's Database, View #2

on the basis of one of the fields. Sorts can be ascending (alphabetical or numbered low to high) or descending (reverse alphabetical or numbered high to low). The ability to conduct multiple sorts encourages students to explore data in a way that is not possible without computers.

Another useful feature of databases is their ability to process numeric data. Any field can be set up to hold numeric data. Fields containing numeric data can be referenced in formulas placed in other numeric fields. For example, if a record includes several fields that contain children's scores on various projects, there can be an additional field that reports the average of all of those numeric fields.

Finally, databases are useful for generating reports in various formats. One way to report data is to simply print all the fields for all the records. Rarely would such a report be useful, however. An alternative is to select specific fields for reporting, sort the database in reference to one of those selected fields, and print a report showing only the fields of interest. The arrangement of the selected fields on the pages of the report can be manipulated on-screen before printing so that the most effective presentation can be created.

How Can Databases Help Teachers?

Excellent teachers keep all kinds of information about their students. Databases provide a convenient way to catalog the information teachers collect about their students. Information such as family background, address and telephone number, birthday, health problems or medications, hobbies, preferred learning style, titles of books read, sports enjoyed, trips taken, and so on, is the type of information that can be kept in an electronic database. The teacher can create a database in which each student has a record and each of these bits of information is stored in a field. If the teacher decides to add an additional field later to each child's record, this can easily be done.

Having all this information in an electronic database may not make the teacher's job any easier than it would be without such a database. If the teacher's class has the usual 25 to 30 students, it might not even seem to be worth the effort to computerize this data. However, over time, each teacher will have contact with hundreds of children. If these records are kept from year to year, eventually the teacher will have a substantial body of data to consult when she is trying to find ways to help a current student. Perhaps a teacher has a student who is easily distracted, and she is trying to find ways to engage this child in learning. She can consult her database, generate a list of all the students she has had previously who had this same difficulty, and check her records to see what particular interventions were especially effective in helping those earlier students. This might give her an idea of something to try with the current student. Since these are data that the teacher herself has accumulated, and since she is using it only to help her current students, there is no need to be concerned about issues of confidentiality concerning the data. In this case the computer is serving to aid the teacher's memory, and it may enable her to see ideas that she would not have seen without this aid.

Another way that a database can be useful to teachers is in the teacher's response to students' written work when the work is personalized. When each student does a unique assignment it is difficult for the teacher to use a generalized scoring rubric to assess these assignments. It is necessary for the teacher to assess the work on an individual basis, and written comments of various aspects of the student's work are appropriate. When the work is a product or performance, or if a final written product is in a published document, it is not possible for the teacher to write comments directly on the student's work. These circumstances combine to create a situation where a database is an appropriate tool to use for assessment.

A database for assessment would be formed by creating records for individual students. The fields might be the following: name, general description of work, type of work, location of work, comments on specific aspects of the work (degree of persuasiveness, clarity of thought, articulation, expression), scores on aspects of the work, and an overall score. With such data entered into the database, a report can be generated for the students. These reports for the students would include all the evaluative comments, all the scores for the various components, and the overall score. The students receive a written report evaluating their work, but their original piece of work is not defaced by the teacher's comments. The teacher might generate a different report for her own use which shows merely a list of student names accompanied by the overall scores for each student. This information could then be placed into the gradebook.

A further way that databases can be useful to teachers involves the simultaneous use of both a database and a word processor. Using these two tools together teachers can create a mailing that goes to all students or all parents and which is personalized for each recipient. The use of this feature of word processing with a database is called "mail merge." The database contains fields for the names and addresses of the recipients. On the word processor the teacher creates a letter that includes special characters and identifiers used as spaceholders where the names and addresses should appear in the letter. These characters and identifiers connect the word processing document to specific fields in a specific database. The word processor then reads the items from the database and creates a copy of the document for each person in the database. As each document is produced, the appropriate entries from the database are supplied.

DELTA PRINCIPLE PERSPECTIVE ON DATABASES

An electronic database used to manage teaching responsibilities can have positive, Level III impacts on teaching. We have already seen how a teacher can use a database to keep and consult student records, to assess individualized assignments, and to create mail-merge word processing documents. A further illustration is presented here showing how one teacher uses an electronic database* to keep track of published ideas, activities, and theories on teaching. This use of a database is one of this teacher's most beneficial professional development resources.

> After five years of teaching, Susan was beginning to feel overwhelmed by the amount of material she was accumulating. Journal articles, research studies, ideas and tips for classroom activities, books on theory, and various newsletters all began to blur together for her. She could never remember where she had read what, and could never find what she needed when she needed it. The things that she used regularly didn't present any problems for her, but she knew that she had read about good ideas and had neglected to use them. She didn't want to keep losing track of good teaching ideas. She always took brief notes on most of what she read, and she filed all of her notes in one specific folder on her computer. But searching for specific notes on specific topics was very time consuming.
>
> Then she heard about an electronic database program that was designed to help people keep track of their professional readings and store the vital information such as author, title, date, source, publisher, and so on. This software even promised to format citations in a paper in any number of formal styles (including APA!). Maybe she could get a paper of her own published in one of her professional journals!

---

*The software described in the vignette is *EndNote Plus*, which is published by Niles and Associates, Inc., 2000 Hearst St., Suite 200, Berkeley, CA 94709.

Susan bought a copy of the software and began using it to take notes on her readings. One of the fields available was for an abstract of what she read. This was her most useful field. She also used cut and paste to transfer her older notes into this database. When she finished transferring her old notes she was amazed to find that she now had a single database with 135 different books, articles, and newsletters documented. She tried out the *search* function. She performed a search for all records that contained the words "authentic assessment." Within seconds the software provided a list of 23 records that contained these words. As she browsed through the abstracts of these 23 records, it was like visiting old friends. Some she remembered well because she had read them recently or had used the ideas regularly. Others she had forgotten about, and re-reading her own abstracts brought them back to mind in a refreshing new look. The next day she decided to use one of the ideas that had been brought back to her memory by this casual search.

Now every time Susan reads or discovers a new resource she adds it to her own personal "library" as she calls it. Her database has grown to contain over 200 entries. She consults it regularly, because now she knows that she doesn't have to remember everything about everything she reads. As a result of her constant use of this database she finds herself being reminded of certain works she's read over and over again. As a result of this constant review, Susan has become somewhat of an authority in her school. Her peers have discovered that she seems to have command of educational literature more than she had before. They come to her with questions about "what the experts say" about various things. When she can't answer their questions, she looks them up in her database. And yes, she has written a paper on authentic assessment, and she is waiting to hear from the journal publishers about whether or not they will publish it!

Perhaps the benefits to Susan's teaching as a result of her use of a special database are obvious. This is a very clear example of how we need to depend on technology to keep us afloat in the "sea of information" that characterizes this Information Age (Naisbitt, 1982).

Without the ability to electronically catalog all the ideas she was finding, Susan was unable to effectively use all of them. By keeping them stored electronically she found that she didn't need to depend on her own memory to retrieve and use important ideas. Instead, she depended on the computer to find things she needed when she needed them.

Some may argue that Susan's ability to remember what she reads will (or has) deteriorated as a result of her dependence on the technology. In one sense this is true. As she reads a new article, little of Susan's attention is now given to remembering what she is reading. She knows that she doesn't need to remember it because the computer will store whatever notes she takes. She knows the computer can search for and find those notes at any point in the future based on a key-word search. However, a surprising and unexpected benefit to Susan is that by repeated use she does, in fact, remember more details of the things she has stored. In a way, the computer is serving Susan as an electronic flashcard that presents her with repetition of important information in a meaningful context. She devotes less of her energy to memorization, but she actually remembers more!

THINK ABOUT

- Is it good or bad that people come to depend on computers as memory-assistance devices the way that Susan in the last section did? How did human learning and thinking change when books replaced oral traditions as a way of passing along bodies of knowledge?

- It takes time to learn to use a spreadsheet or a database fluently. Is this investment of time worthwhile? What are some of the reasons you think the way you do?

- Some teachers claim that they are getting along just fine without these tools. Do you agree with their thinking? What arguments could you present to try to change the mind of someone who feels differently about this than you do?

- What are some negative effects of using databases and/or spreadsheets that were not discussed in this chapter?

SELECTED REFERENCES

Naisbitt, J. (1982). *Megatrends.* New York: Warner. Naisbitt describes our current situation as one in which more and more information is available, but it is harder and harder to find what we need when we need it.

Ploger, D., Klingler, L., and Rooney, M. (1997). "Spreadsheets, patterns, and algebraic thinking." *Teaching Children Mathematics,* 3(6), 330–334. The authors provide a number of activities that make use of spreadsheets in the elementary grades.

6 Enhancing Social Studies Teaching with Technology

LOOKING AHEAD

Entering the gymnasium on the night of the Social Studies Fair, the visitor was struck by the sights, sounds, and smells of the many displays. A quick scan around the room revealed flags of many colors, children wearing a variety of international clothing, many and varied forms of music, and a dizzying variety of food samples. A closer look around showed maps, travel brochures, hand-crafted articles, money samples, musical instruments, and a multitude of artifacts from around the world. As the visitor wandered from display to display and paused to talk with the children, he realized the wonderful effect this project had had on the learners. It seemed as if each one had become immersed in the culture of the country (s)he had been studying. Some had learned bits and pieces of the language that was native to the country under study. All were thoroughly motivated to share the knowledge that they had gained about the country they were presenting. The visitor wondered where all of the time and energy had come from in order for the children to have produced such an impressive show. The year was 1980; there was not a single computer in the school.

Entering the gymnasium on the night of the Social Studies Fair, the visitor was struck by the sights, sounds, and smells of the many displays. A quick scan around the room revealed flags of many colors, children wearing a variety of international clothing, many and varied forms of music, and a dizzying variety of food samples. A closer look around showed computer-generated maps and banners, travel brochures, hand-crafted articles, money samples, musical instruments, artifacts from around the world, as well as print-outs of e-mail exchanges between the children and their international keypals. As the visitor wandered from display to display and paused to talk with the children, he realized the wonderful effect this project had had on the learners. Many of the children stood by continuously running computer slide presentations that they had composed. Some children were on-line with international friends in a live chat-room. It seemed as if each child had become immersed in the culture of the country (s)he had been studying. Most had learned bits and pieces of the language that was native to the country under study. All were thoroughly motivated to share the knowledge that they had gained about the country they were presenting. The visitor wondered where all of the time and energy had come from in order for the children to have produced such an impressive show. The year was 2000. Nearly every display used a computer or displayed a computer-generated product.

At first glance one might say that the computer has not had a great effect on social studies teaching in the last 20 years or so. After all, in our illustration, great teaching of social studies in 1980 doesn't seem that different from great teaching of social studies in the year 2000. Perhaps the computer is not as powerful a tool for teaching social studies as it is for teaching other subjects. Perhaps social studies is a safe haven for the technophobic teacher.

Such a conclusion would be faulty for several reasons. First and foremost, in the last 20 years the computer has moved into the forefront as one of the most powerful influences on today's society. This alone provides an inescapable mandate to at least study computers in the context of social studies. Secondly, although good social studies teaching today looks a lot like good social studies teaching of the past, the technology today makes such teaching much more accessible than it was in the past. The sights and sounds, at least, of the world are only a few mouseclicks away, whereas in the past the teacher had to do considerable legwork to gather an impressive collection of materials. Thirdly, the goals of social studies usually include some exposure to the methods used by social scientists. Today's social scientists rely heavily on the computer to carry out their research. If the computer were neglected in the teaching of social studies, a very skewed picture would result. Finally, the Internet makes possible the kinds of global connections and interactions that were extremely difficult and impractical in the past. The effects of such interactions among children are probably more profound than we can imagine.

In this chapter we examine many of the ways in which technology is being used to help with the teaching of social studies. We examine how some of the software productivity tools described in chapters 4 and 5 can have specific application in the teaching of social studies. We look at some educational software designed with social studies teaching in mind. We examine how the World Wide Web has become an excellent resource for enhancing social studies teaching. And finally, we consider technology and social studies teaching in light of the Delta Principle.

CAN YOU?

- Describe a social studies project that could be enhanced through the use of a computer database?

- Identify some benefits to children of using databases for studying social studies?

- Describe the TimeLiner program and how it might be used?

- Tell how to use a program such as *Decisions, Decisions* to enhance social studies teaching?

- Suggest ways to use simulation game software as a large-group activity?

- Distinguish between the two primary uses of videodisc software in the social studies classroom?

- Create a project idea that might be suitable for inclusion in the KIDLINK home page?

- Highlight the major features of the National Geographic Kids Network and tell how this network might be used in an elementary classroom?

- Envision a technology-dependent social studies classroom?

TEACHER LABORATORY

Before you read this chapter it would be a good idea to clarify what we mean when we address *social studies.* Write down a definition of *social studies.* Note that the word is plural. In your definition identify the various disciplines that you believe are included in the social studies. Obtain a textbook for methods of teaching social studies and compare your definition with the one given in that text. How close were you? What aspects did you omit? What aspects did you identify that were not in the textbook definition?

USING THE TOOLS

General Databases

Teachers have sometimes used visits to old cemeteries for a study of history. Children would take rubbings of the gravestones in order to collect information on people who lived in another time. This activity is well-suited for use with database software. A computer database can be easily set up to store information on names and dates found on the gravestones. A calculation field can be used to determine the person's age at the time of their death. If a laptop computer is available the teacher can enter the data on-site during the class's visit.

In order to help the children bring history to life, the database can be used to explore interesting questions about particular peri-

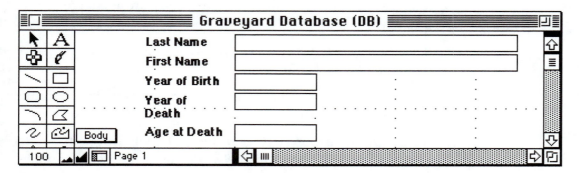

Figure 6–1.   The Layout of the Graveyard Database

Last Name	First Name	Year of Birth	Age at Death
Altone	Rachel	1799	73
Altone	John	1799	81
Altone	Peter	1822	81
Bonner	Luke	1842	46
Bonner	Rebecca	1850	42
March	Anne	1859	41
Bonner	Suzanne	1860	0
Richards	James	1863	82
Richards	Amy	1870	95
Struthers	Nathan	1880	62
Petty	Martha	1903	19

Graveyard Database (DB)

Records: 11

Sorted

Figure 6–2.   The Graveyard Database; columnar layout

ods in time. For example, if the data are sorted into alphabetical order by last name, the children can speculate about which people were related to one another. If a layout containing names, dates of birth, and ages is examined, it may become evident which people were husband and wife and which people may have been children of those couples. This same layout makes it obvious which people were children who died in childhood. Students can be taught to pose and answer their own interesting questions while examining this database. Using the computer's ability to match records according to Boolean logical operators, children can be taught to find people who might have died in battle in specific wars. They can create life stories of the people they are studying containing such speculations as who might have known whom and how these people might have reacted to the current events of their day. The ease with which a database allows children to explore their own questions makes this an ideal tool for exploring history. At the same time it provides an authentic context in which the teacher can teach the skills of using a computerized database.

The following vignette illustrates how some fifth-graders used the graveyard database to explore their own questions.

Sudha: I've heard that a lot of children died young back in the 1800s. I wonder if that's true here? I wonder how we can find out?

Rebecca: We can just look down through the list of their ages at the time of death. That would tell us.

Sudha: I know, but there are hundreds of them to look through. Maybe we can get it to just show us the children.

Rebecca: What if we have it sort the database using age? Then we'd have all the children listed at the beginning!

Sudha: Yes, that's great! Let's do it!

Sudha: Wow! Look at all the babies that died! There must be dozens of kids under age two!

Rebecca: And look, after about age 4 not too many people died until about age 45, then there are more again.

Sudha: So, it looks like if you lived to be age 4 you would probably make it to be an adult.

Rebecca: Wait a minute. We wanted to find out if more children died young in the 1800s, but we've got people in here that lived in the 1900s. They're all mixed in together. How can we tell if more babies died in the 1800s than in the 1900s?

Sudha: We can look at the dates of death along with the ages.

Rebecca: Yeah, but like you said earlier, maybe there's a way to have the computer sort them out for us. Let's ask Mrs. Conklin.

The children get their teacher's attention and ask her how to accomplish their goal.

Mrs. Conklin: There are different ways to do what you want to do. Since you've already got the data listed in order of age at death, the easiest thing would be to have the computer highlight the records that are from the nineteenth century. From the

Organize menu, choose Match Records.* Then put in a formula that says, 'Year of Death' < 1900. This will highlight all the records that have a year of death that is smaller than 1900. Then you can browse through and look at the highlighted records.

Sudha: OK, let's try it. Yes! I was right! Look—most of the babies that died were from the 1800s. I wonder why that is?

There are a few things to note about this vignette. First of all, there is an emphasis on the children posing their own questions. Children who are able to pose and investigate their own questions are working on a much higher cognitive level than are children who are merely responding to someone else's questions. Technology such as an interesting computerized database makes it easier to give children an opportunity for such explorations. Secondly, it is clear that the children have received enough training in the use of the database that they know when it is possible to have the computer help them with their questions. They *could* have just looked through the data to find low ages of death, but they realized that a simple sort of the database would make their job easier. This kind of knowledge is not innate. The children have been exposed to databases enough that they are beginning to base their explorations on the capabilities of the database. They are well on their way to Delta Level III in their use of data. Finally, when they need more skills than they presently have it is appropriate for the teacher to provide direct instruction to help them explore their question. The teacher took advantage of a "teachable moment" to provide some instruction in a more advanced level of skill in database use.

Specialized Databases

Another kind of database that is particularly well-suited to teaching social studies are the commercial databases that hold geographic and demographic data on all the major countries in the world. An example of such a program is *MacGlobe* from Broderbund software. Such programs have statistics, charts, and maps on such topics as population, land area, major landforms, major religions, income

---

*The example uses ClarisWorks 4.0 menus and terminology.

levels, major exports and imports, average life expectancy, and so on. Such programs often are shipped with teachers' manuals that provide suggested activities and curriculum projects. Unfortunately, most often these guides lack vision in terms of how to best use the technological power of the product. For example, a typical activity for *MacGlobe* might be to "locate two countries that are intersected by the line of 15° S latitude." Such tasks involve low-level thinking skills and could just as easily be performed without the benefit of technology.

The technological power of a database such as *MacGlobe* is its ability to display data in a variety of formats and in a way that facilitates comparisons. For example, health data on countries in Central America are available in the form of maps (see Figure 6–3) or graphs (see Figure 6–4). The same data are also available in tabular form for individual countries (see Figure 6–5). A learning task that engages students in making use of such data in an authentic problem-finding setting would be a suitable use of technology. An

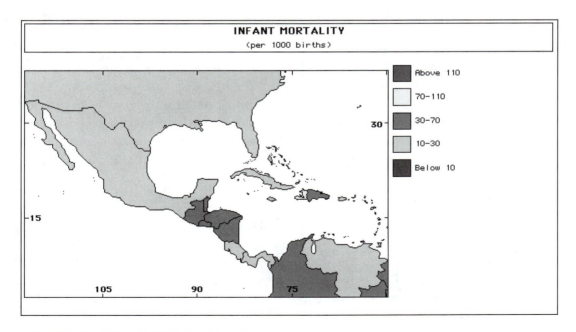

Figure 6–3.   Map of Central America's Infant Mortality

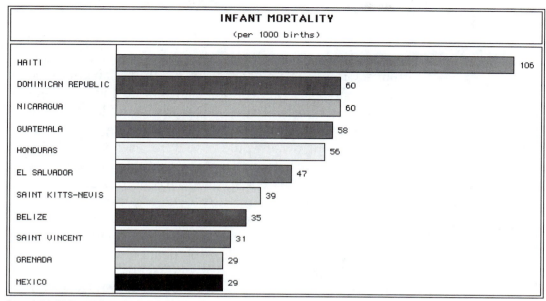

Figure 6–4.   Graph of Central America's Infant Mortality

HAITI

HEALTH STATISTICS

Life Expectancy (Male):	52 yrs
Life Expectancy (Female):	55 yrs
Crude Birth Rate:	43/1000
Crude Death Rate:	15/1000
Infant Mortality:	106/1000

	NUMBER	POP'N PER
Hospitals	87	72,264
Hospital Beds	4,566	1,377
Physicians	944	6,660
Dentists	98	64,153
Pharmacists	6	1,047,833
Nurses	657	9,569

Figure 6–5.   Table of Haiti's Health Statistics

example of such a learning task is described in the following extended description.

The teacher has divided the class into five learning groups. Group 1 is a medical team, Group 2 is an education team, Group 3 is an agricultural team, Group 4 is a tourism-development team, and Group 5 is an industrial-development team. Each team is assigned the task of finding one Central American country that would benefit from an extended visit from that particular team. They must find and examine the available data on the Central American countries and plan an extended visit to that country to provide assistance.

The teacher uses direct instruction to show the students how to use *MacGlobe* to display "country reports" for the Central American nations showing data on selected topics. The class decides together which topics would be most helpful for their particular needs. (They choose reports on health statistics; resources, agriculture and industries; culture and tourism; education; agricultural products; and manufactured goods.) The teacher also shows them how to produce maps and graphs that provide the same data in country-by-country comparison format.

Prior to using the computers, the students are directed to identify what are the strengths and resources of their teams. Their task is to define the kinds of problems that they think they are best equipped to solve. As soon as this is done, they are permitted to begin searching the database to find a country that they feel will benefit most from their talents. Since the classroom has five computers, each team uses one computer for this portion of the task.

The medical team decides that they are best equipped to provide health care such as vaccinations, surgeries, and medical education. They begin by browsing through the health maps for all the Central American countries. By the time they get to the infant mortality map, the country in yellow has attracted their attention. They drag the cursor over it to find out what country it is. As the cursor is dragged over this country they discover that it is Haiti. They next examine the graph for infant mortality and discover that Haiti has the highest rate of infant mortality of all the Central American countries. They decide to examine Haiti's country report to see what their other health statistics look like. They decide that Haiti is the country that needs them the most, and they report this to their teacher. The teacher urges them to do a more thorough comparison before arriving at this conclusion. After comparing Haiti to the other Central American countries on all available health statistics, the team is certain that Haiti is the place they need to go. Each of the teams arrives at a conclusion by the end of the first day of work on this task.

The next day the teacher asks the teams to identify some tourist attractions that they would like to visit while they are in the country of their choice. She also asks them to find out what requirements will need to be met in terms of visas and health immunizations. She asks them to identify a time of year that they would like to visit. She asks them to determine how far they will have to travel to get to the capital city of their country if they leave from New York City. She asks them to determine what currency they will need. Finally she asks them what their plan will be to help the country alleviate the problem that they have identified. All the answers to these questions are to be written up as a proposed travel plan and submitted to the entire class for their approval. The teams will have two class periods to develop their proposals.

On the fourth day of class the teacher asks each group to present their proposals to the entire group. After each proposal is presented, the class votes on whether or not to approve the plans. Any teams whose plans are not approved must be given specific guidelines for how to improve the plans.

Everything that is required in order to carry out this learning task is available in the *MacGlobe* database. The teacher could extend this project by having the students research the cost of transportation, food, and accommodations. The important feature of this learning activity is that it uses the power of technology to challenge the students to the highest levels of thinking. The children will be involved in truly constructivist learning as they pose problems, locate, analyze and evaluate data, and synthesize action plans. Such dynamic learning activities are possible but much more difficult without the use of technology. However, the technology itself, in this case a specialized database, does not ensure this kind of dynamic learning.

Timeliner

A specialized tool program produced and marketed by Tom Snyder Productions is *Timeliner*. *Timeliner* is used to generate timelines and other displays that make use of proportionally segmented visual space. A user of the program enters data (events and dates) into a table and the software converts that data into a correctly proportioned timeline. The user can be the teacher, if (s)he wants to make a timeline for the class to study, or it may be a student or a group of students working on a project. Graphics may be included in the timeline. The timeline format can be horizontal or vertical.

The creator of the timeline can choose to compress or expand the scale, resulting in a timeline that fits on a single 8.5" by 11" paper or one that requires dozens of pages. Students who explore the timeline before it is printed can gain an understanding of the perspective of history by viewing the timeline with varying degrees of compression. Events that happened close together in time can appear to be quite spread out if a greatly expanded scale is used. On the other hand, these events can appear to be almost simultaneous if a compressed scale is used. The dramatic difference caused by adjusting the scale is a valuable learning experience, and it will help children to become more critical users of timelines.

Creative teachers have discovered that *Timeliner* can be used for purposes other than timelines. One teacher entered the distances of the planets from the sun, and the program produced a scale drawing of the solar system. (This drawing showed the distances but not the sizes of the planets in the correct scale.) Teachers of geography can use this capability of *Timeliner* to produce scale models of local distances that are of interest to the students.

USING EDUCATIONAL SOFTWARE

There are several different types of software available to support the teaching of social studies. Some of them offer no particular benefits over text or workbooks, and therefore, the cost is not usually justified. The following pieces of software, however, offer an interesting and/or powerful advantage, and they have stood the test of time. These titles could almost be considered "classics" in the teaching of social studies.

Decisions, Decisions

Tom Snyder Productions has developed an entire collection of software modeled after the successful *Decisions, Decisions* programs. This software is used to promote dialog and group decision-making in the classroom. The learning occurs as a result of the interactions that the software promotes among the students and between the students and the teacher. The software presents a simulation/vignette in which a series of choices must be made. The teacher reads or presents the simulation, stopping it at the point of decision. The class is then split into small groups to discuss the alternatives and come to a consensus. The small groups then report to the whole class and an attempt is made to create a consensus among all members of the class. The teacher then enters the class's consensus decision and the simulation proceeds. The course of the simulation is determined by the option selected by the class. Eventually another decision point is reached, and the cycle repeats. Each decision point affects the progress and eventual outcome of the simulation.

David Dockterman (1997), one of the authors of the *Decisions, Decisions* series, describes the way he likes to use the software. He uses a "layered" approach to the decision-making in which individuals make their own informed decisions, and then these individuals work in groups of four to develop a small-group consensus, and then these small groups present their opinions to the whole class. In the end the class decision is generally made by voting. In order to promote thoughtful discussion among the children, the software comes with class sets of four different "advisor" books. Each member of the four-person small groups gets one of the advisor books. These books contain conflicting positions on each of the issues faced, and they provide facts and historical perspectives that the children would probably not know on their own. The group members each read to the group the relevant material from their advisor books, and the children can use this material in formulating their arguments to the others. When the children are presenting their positions to the class, Dockterman usually acts as devil's advocate to get them to think about perspectives that they had ignored. He does this in order to help the children become aware of the complexity and ambiguity that are involved in today's social issues. Using computers in this way provides an emphasis on wisdom. It is a good way to prevent some of the unintended negative effects of technology that Monke (1997) warns of.

Although this software is technically quite simple, and the model of teaching that it promotes is certainly possible without the use of a computer, *Decisions, Decisions* makes this kind of teaching much easier than it would otherwise be. This type of software promotes such social studies goals as understanding democracy, participatory citizenship, persuasive speaking, and critical thinking. Some of the topics that are presented through the *Decisions, Decisions* software are *Ancient Empires, Balancing the Budget, The Cold War, Colonization,* and *Feudalism.* As of November, 1997, there were 17 different titles designed for use in grades 5 through 12.

The Oregon Trail

The Oregon Trail is probably the best-known of many geographical/historical simulation games that are available. In this game the player takes the role of a pioneer setting out with a wagon train from St. Louis and destined for the coast of Oregon in the mid-nineteenth century. Decisions must be made about what occupation to have, how much food and ammunition to bring along, how many horses or oxen to purchase, and so on. Along the way the pioneer deals with weather problems, diminishing food supply, illnesses, and hunting and trading difficulties. Every decision the player makes has a bearing on the kinds of difficulties faced, and ultimately, on whether or not the trip is successful. This game allows the player to experience some of the facets of life faced by the pioneers that made this dangerous journey. In the newest CD-ROM versions of this software there are educational and motivating video and audio clips to give background on the history and geography of the Oregon Trail.

Use of this game (and games like it) in the classroom should go beyond simply providing time for the children to play the game on their own. One way to use the game to support the curriculum is to help children learn about the five geography themes of Location, Place, Relationships within Place, Movement, and Region (National Council for Geographic Education, 1994) through the use of this game. Some teachers have created learning centers using the computer and *Oregon Trail* as the major component of the center. Along with the game is a notebook containing questions and activities designed to help the children learn about the geography themes. For example: on the theme of movement, children are asked to keep track of how long it takes them to make the trip from St. Louis to the Oregon coast. Reference books are provided and the children are asked to compare the time it took them in the game to the time it took groups led by Marcus and Narcissa Whitman. These times are then compared to today's travel times for the same route as calculated by the children through the use of maps and calculators. Children are asked to compare the benefits and disadvantages of today's travel methods with those methods of earlier times. Children respond to questions about issues such as environmental and social costs of today's automobiles and highway systems, and they make judgments about whether the costs are worth the benefits.

The *Carmen Sandiego* Series

Originating with the application titled *Where in the World Is Carmen Sandiego?*, an entire line of simulation software has been developed around the idea of tracking and capturing criminals. Using this software, children learn to use an almanac and other reference books, they learn to use maps, they learn to make judgments about the relevancy of information they find, they learn facts about history and geography, they develop their problem-solving skills, and they have fun doing so. In each game the software presents a simulated situation in which a crime has been committed and the child playing the game is the detective assigned to capture the crook. The software contains background information on several possible suspects and as the game progresses it provides clues that can be used to help the child identify the criminal. The child must follow the clues as the criminal travels around the globe (and in some games through time as well!). As more bits of evidence are discovered and compared with the background information on the suspects, the child can use logical deduction to determine who committed the crime. If enough evidence is gathered the child can obtain a warrant for the arrest of a certain suspect. The game is timed. If the child catches up with the criminal before time runs out, and if the child has a warrant for the correct person, the criminal is apprehended and the crime is solved. As a child solves a number of crimes, (s)he receives periodic promotions to higher and higher ranks as a detective.

It is through interpreting the clues in these games that the child's history and geography learning are enhanced. Clues might be related to coins, currency, or flags from various countries. The children would use an almanac to look up information to help them decode the clues. Clues might be related to historical events, and students would use a reference book to look up further information on those events in order to decode the clues. One way to use the games is as a supplement to the regular curriculum. Children might be permitted the opportunity to play the game as a part of a learning center when they had free time.

A more compelling way to use the game is to make it an integral part of the curriculum. One of the games is *Where in America's Past Is Carmen Sandiego?* If the curriculum centers around American history, the use of this game can provide vital support. Some teachers have used the game with their classes by having the class act together as the detective. Decisions about what clues to follow or where to go to look for more clues are handled by small groups of children who take turns giving their responses. When one group is deliberating about the next choice, the other groups work on charts to place in the classroom stating what they have learned about American history during the course of the game. The game is played in this way periodically (perhaps once or twice a week), and over time an impressive array of charts is posted around the room. When the game is used in this way the class is the recipient of each promotion, and the children enjoy seeing their progress as they corporately obtain a higher and higher rank.

Using Videodisc Software

Although science is the subject most strongly supported by videodisc software, there are some excellent videodiscs available to enhance social studies teaching. As with science, there are essentially two ways to use videodiscs in the classroom: The teacher can create video presentations that are enhanced by and dependent on selected video clips, or the students can explore the video information on their own. Both uses require a HyperCard (or similar) program to provide controlled access to the material on the videodisc.

ABC News has produced some videodisc titles that are of interest to the social studies teacher. One title, *In the Holy Land,* is a video exploration of the political and religious forces that are behind the ongoing tension between Israel and Palestine. Glencoe is another company that produces videodiscs. Their *Set on Freedom: The American Civil Rights Movement* includes some historic video footage from the 1960s. *History in Motion* is a videodisc set that was produced by Scholastic. A number of videodiscs have been produced by the Smithsonian Institution. One of these that has particular importance for the social studies teacher is the *First Ladies* collection. It provides an inside look at the Smithsonian Institution's collection of articles related to the First Ladies. In addition to the wealth of video information, there is much indexed textual information about the First Ladies as well.

For younger elementary children the primary value in these videodisc collections is in teacher-made presentations. The hours of video on each disc are far too long and involved for young audiences. However, the teacher can select several pertinent short clips and use these to tell a story. Because the video images are high quality, and because the teacher can put the clips together in a way that will interest her own students, this can be a powerful teaching tool in some situations.

For older elementary and middle school students these videodisc collections can be used in far different ways. For these older students the collections are best used as a resource for materials to be included in student-made multimedia presentations. As the Apple Classroom of Tomorrow (Dwyer, 1994) project has shown, when young people have access to abundant technology they can learn to collaborate on complex and sophisticated multimedia projects. The video footage on these videodisc collections and the HyperCard stacks that provide control over them are powerful tools in the hands of a creative and motivated group of young people.

We have found that students respond well when they are given an initial period of time without any particular directions in which to explore what these collections contain. After an initial exploration period the students should be required to pose several questions or problems that they might like to explore in depth. These questions or problems should be discussed with the teacher who can help the students refine them into a single statement of project goals. A part of the project goals should always be to identify divergent perspectives and evaluate the materials for bias. (One of the dangers in using powerful multimedia is that the students often neglect to notice that the materials may be biased.) After writing a statement of project goals, the students will take responsibilities for various components of the task. Someone may take responsibility for *locating* pertinent video footage. Someone else may take responsibility for finding appropriate *text* information to support the project. Someone else may take responsibility for *organizing* the material that is gathered so that it supports a thematic presentation. All the students should become involved in assembling the final multimedia presentation. One of the students may be interested in actually *presenting* the finished product to an audience. Possibly the presentation will be of high enough quality that it can be published on the World Wide Web.

USING THE WORLD WIDE WEB

The World Wide Web perhaps has more to offer to social studies teachers than to teachers of any other subject. Some of the major goals of social studies teaching, such as developing an understanding of other cultures and other places, fit naturally with the resources of the web. Through the web, children are developing friendships with children from all corners of the globe. These friendships serve to give the children firsthand, peer-appropriate accounts of the different cultures and places. Children from around the world can engage in dialog on important topics. Today's children can have daily or nearly-daily communications with other children on nearly every continent. Through collaborative classroom projects, classes of children can work together with other classes thousands of miles away. The resources of the web are truly unique when it comes to social studies teaching. The kinds of collaboration and communication that are possible with the web are not possible through any other avenues.

KIDLINK

KIDLINK was introduced in chapter 3 as an example of an organization that sponsors Internet Relay Chats for young people. KIDLINK has many other projects in addition to the IRC project. The overall goal of the KIDLINK organization is to promote global dialog among young people. (At the time of this writing, participation was restricted to young people 10 to 15 years old, but debate was underway about removing this age restriction.) Students who want to participate in KIDLINK must register by answering four questions: (1) *Who am I?* (giving information on name, age, gender, home location, and school), (2) *What do I want to be when I grow up?*, (3) *How do I want the world to be better when I grow up?*, and (4) *What can I do now to make this happen?*. After answering these questions young people may join in any of the projects that are currently underway. Teacher-leaders of KIDLINK announce projects and solicit involvement through the KIDLINK web page (http://www.kidlink.org). Communication among project leaders, project participants, and other interested persons takes place behind the scenes in a number of KIDLINK listservs. Each listserv has a specific purpose: one is for discussion about IRC, one is for discussion of projects, one is for discussion of policies, and so on.

It is impossible to provide an adequate idea of the scope of KIDLINK projects in a text of this sort. The reader is strongly urged to visit the KIDLINK web page and explore some of the current projects. To give some flavor of what can be found there, however, we provide the following description. The Family History Project is a project that was initiated in Fall of 1997. Some of the goals of the project are as follows:

- To bring history alive for students by assisting them in learning how their family participated in 'real' history

- To learn how previous generations actually lived, values they had, customs they practiced, etc.

- To promote creative writing skills

- To develop research and note-taking skills by "digging" around in the family tree

- To learn about other cultures by sharing with each other on the Kidproj list

- To increase computer skills by using word processors, perhaps drawing or graphics programs, e-mail, listservs, and the WWW

- To learn more about community resources in individual geographical areas

Participants are encouraged to begin the project by interviewing the oldest member of their family to uncover some interesting pieces of the family's history. (At http://www.rootsweb.com/~genepool/oralhist.htm there is a list of dozens of suitable interview questions.) Some families have a family Bible or other written or photographic artifacts that may contribute to an understanding of family history. The goal in the beginning stages of the project is for students to put together a data bank of personal family information. The organizers of the project provide clear guidance for how to create a *family record sheet* for organizing and keeping track of family data. The project makes extensive use of genealogical research tools and resources that are available on the web. Students learn to use the same tools and techniques that "real" genealogical researchers use.

Once the students have the beginnings of a database of family history information, they are encouraged to pose questions and submit them to the Kidproj list. With the help of adult volunteers the students learn how to conduct further research to uncover answers to their own questions. A part of the project involves having the students write about their family history and share what they've written on a special listserv devoted to the Family History Project. Writing prompts are provided, including "What values does your family believe in so much that they sacrificed a lot for them?" and "Tell family stories that show your family's connection to the land." Such writing prompts provide a potent interdisciplinary activity that has both language arts and social studies value. The Family History Project provides much guidance, but it is also quite open-ended. The teacher could choose to remain in the project for an extended period of time, or (s)he could use it for specific limited purposes. When one considers the fact that the Family History Project is one of a dozen or more current projects available through

KIDLINK, the value of KIDLINK as an educational resource becomes evident.

National Geographic Kids Network

Originally funded by the National Science Foundation, and developed by the National Geographic Society and the Technical Education Research Center in Cambridge, Massachusetts, National Geographic Kids Network is an excellent example of on-line education that supports social studies learning. This curriculum project is actually a cross-disciplinary project that supports science learning as well as social studies learning. In this project children participate in one of several different units of instruction. The *Hello!* unit introduces the class to the use of the NGS Kids Network concepts and software. The content units are titled *Weather in Action, Acid Rain, Too Much Trash, What's in Our Water?, What Are We Eating?*, and *Solar Energy.* In each of these units the class is assigned to a research team composed of several geographically dispersed schools. The children in each school gather and record data, send the data to a central computer, and receive an analysis of all the data from the team schools. The data analysis is provided by a scientist assigned to work with the team schools.

In the *Hello!* unit "students find their own school's latitude and longitude location, enter them into the computer, and later send this information to the central NGK computer. Through the network they learn the global address of each of the schools on their research team. In this way they are introduced to the fundamentals of geography" (*Hello!* Teacher Guide). In another Hello activity, students conduct a survey to find out the number and kinds of pets they own. They record this data and send it to the other schools in their research teams. They are later able to retrieve data from schools on their research teams. The students learn to use the NGK software to compile and view the data as tables, charts, and graphs. Other topics that are shared in the *Hello!* unit are climate, landscape, economy, population, transportation, and entertainment features.

The *Hello!* unit is a preparation for the activities in the *Acid Rain* unit. In the *Acid Rain* unit they learn about pH and how to measure it. Later they collect data on the pH of their rainwater. They send this data to the central computer where a research scientist analyzes the data and sends a report to each participating school. The children learn to use maps to plot the locations of the participating schools. They also place the pH data on the maps and use information from the scientist to interpret the data. The maps are helpful in determining causes for variations in pH levels. This exploration helps children discover the relationships between environment and culture (relationships within place), which as cited earlier is one of the five fundamental themes for study of geography.

The materials for the National Geographic Kids Network units are well-designed and helpful. There are teachers' guides, software diskettes, handouts, and student booklets. The materials are aimed at teaching social studies and science, and the computer is a tool that is used in the process.

DELTA PRINCIPLE PERSPECTIVE

Much of the educational software described in this chapter was designed to enhance social studies teaching. The discussions generated by *Decisions, Decisions* and the taste of reality provided by *Oregon Trail* and the Carmen Sandiego series are enhancements to the traditional social studies curriculum. They represent Delta Level I uses of educational technology. They are unlikely to be the catalyst for changes in the way children learn social studies. Certainly they make learning social studies more fun and interesting. They probably open social studies learning to students with a wider range of learning styles and intelligences than would have been possible otherwise. But it seems unlikely that they will cause us to redefine social studies teaching.

Videodiscs in the social studies classroom can represent a Delta Level III use of technology if they are used as a resource by children making their own multimedia presentations. The possibility of children conducting research to locate and use video footage to help them communicate their knowledge is a powerful possibility. In order to assemble an effective video report students will have to view a fairly large quantity of video footage and make evaluative judgments about what to use and what to ignore. As they create a video report they will need to be aware of how their viewers will synthesize knowledge from their presentation. To the extent that such activities begin to *define* learning in social studies, children's concept of social studies learning will change. Since so much of today's current events are learned through television it has become very important for children to learn what is involved in composing a visual report. It is appropriate for the next generation of learners to begin to define social studies partly in terms of visual presentations. The danger that teachers must guard against is children who would tend to define social studies too narrowly. Becoming aware of the issues behind the visual presentations involves reflective thinking. If the use of video presentations fosters reflective thinking, the effect of the technology will have been beneficial. If the use of video distracts from reflective thinking, then the use of the technology will have been harmful. Whether the technology is beneficial or harmful seems to depend on the teacher's handling of the deeper issues.

Another Level III use of technology will be the kinds of Internet projects that we have described here. These projects represent an area that has no parallel among other technologies. There is no substitute for instantaneous communication and collaboration among global learning partners. Of all the things described and imagined in this text, this seems to have the greatest potential to dramatically change the way children learn and think about the world. Rather than having foreign countries represented by pictures and narrative in texts, today's children can have foreign countries represented by relationships with peers in those countries. Where teachers of a few years ago had to struggle to make other nations real to their students, today's teachers can orchestrate real international friendships and interdependence. It is difficult not to be enthusiastic about the possibilities this opens for children's learning.

THINK ABOUT

- What are some of the problems or difficulties with teaching social studies? Which of these problems are well-suited to technological solutions? Which ones will remain in spite of technology? What new problems will arise as technology becomes more prevalent in the teaching of social studies?

SELECTED REFERENCES

Brophy, J. and Alleman, J. (1996). *Powerful social studies for elementary students.* Fort Worth, TX: Harcourt Brace College Publishers.

Chapin, J. K. and Messick, R. (1996). *Elementary social studies: A practical guide* (3rd ed). White Plains, NY: Longman.

Dockterman, D. (1997). *Great teaching in the one computer classroom* (4th ed.). Watertown, MA: Tom Snyder Productions.

Dwyer, D. (1994). "Apple classrooms of tomorrow: What we've learned." *Educational Leadership,* 51(April), 4–10.

Monke, L. (1997). "The web & the plow: Putting the computer in its place." *Teacher Magazine* (October), 30–34.

National Council for Geographic Education (1994). *Geography for life: National geography standards 1994.* Washington, DC: National Geographic Society.

Saxe, D. W. (1994). *Social studies for the elementary teacher.* Boston: Allyn and Bacon.

Turner, T. (1999). *Essentials of elementary social studies* (2nd ed.). Boston: Allyn and Bacon.

7 Enhancing Science Teaching with Technology

LOOKING AHEAD

"Students shouldn't be looking at a screen! They need to be involved with the real world. Hands-on experience is the best way to learn science. Give kids some simple lab equipment and let them examine the real world, not some imitation of reality."

How do you respond to this kind of comment? Doesn't it make a lot of sense? As is true in many situations, there is a lot of truth in the argument. But the fundamental flaw in the logic is the belief that the options are either to observe the real world or else work exclusively in an artificial simulation. There is actually a synergistic effect, the whole being greater than the sum of the parts, when real world measurements are combined with computer-based analysis. In this chapter, we will look at a few of the many ways technology can help youngsters learn about science. There will only be space to look at a couple of them. But we'll also do something that is perhaps more important—we will explore ways to tap into an essentially unlimited amount of information that can guide you for years to come as you design science lessons that take advantage of the latest technologies.

CAN YOU?

- Show students the basic operation of a spreadsheet for calculating and making graphs?

- Set up a simple database to keep track of your lessons and supplementary material?

- Describe some of the different types of CD-ROM packages that are available for the elementary classroom?

- Select a series of images or movie clips from a videodisc that would be helpful in a science lesson?

- Imagine how your students could utilize a microcomputer-based lab probe for an open house display?

- "Surf the web" in an efficient manner to locate other teachers who are trying to use technology in their elementary science lessons?

TEACHER LABORATORY

Pick out a vendor of science equipment appropriate for your classroom and see if you can locate the manufacturer's web-site. A good way to start would be to simply type the company's name as a URL into your web browser. For example, if you were looking for computer equipment, just typing the word "Apple" (without the quotes) is enough to link you directly to that company's huge collection of web pages. If entering the name of your favorite vendor does not work, try using one of the Internet Search Engines that are available.

USING THE TOOLS

What is it about technology that makes it so hard to apply in the classroom? Probably the biggest obstacle is just deciding what you want to do! Today's computers are so powerful that they can accomplish a seemingly unlimited number of tasks. Like being in a room with five doors on every wall, it's difficult to know which portal to open. There are straightforward instructional lessons, tool software like spreadsheets, data collection hardware, and of course, the Internet. Since there is no way we could cover all these possibilities, let alone predict what new ones might come along next year, we've decided to present a few general approaches and then show you how you can learn more and keep up to date with this fast-changing area.

Productivity Software

Any businessperson can relate the value of using spreadsheets. These programs are so useful that it's hard to find a computer that doesn't have some kind of spreadsheet program already stored on its hard disk. It may be difficult to see how these business-oriented packages can be useful for elementary students, and some will argue that you shouldn't even allow children who are just developing their basic arithmetic skills to use them. We agree that students need to memorize things like multiplication tables to survive as adults. But they should also become familiar with the powerful technological tools they will probably use when they grow up. Beyond this pragmatic view, there are important pedagogical reasons for showing youngsters how to use spreadsheets. The real power of these packages is their ability to help analyze "what if . . ." scenarios. Students can collect information on a topic of interest to them and then use a spreadsheet to graph their findings. They can then carry their analysis farther and see what happens if they change some of the numbers. Certainly they need to know how to carry out the calculations by hand. But having to repeat exactly the same type of analysis 30 or 40 times can quickly take the fun out of mathematics and completely obscure the original reason for doing the computation. A spreadsheet can make hundreds of calculations easily and perhaps help students see some of the exciting things you can do with mathematics. If you were teaching sixth graders about averages, you could have them set up a spreadsheet as an "Averaging Machine." You could make a classroom game out of calling out numbers and having students guess what the average would be. They could then quickly check out their guess with the "Machine." This little exercise not only helps them see the power of spreadsheets and how averages are calculated, it also helps them build an intuitive understanding of the math concept.

Databases can also be extremely useful tools. Don't think that all you can do with these organizers is keep track of your students' addresses and phone numbers. For example, let's say you are trying to develop a lesson on the solar system. Rather than sitting down with a couple books and making up a worksheet for your students, imagine the following possibility:

Mr. Holmes: OK class, it's almost time to head to the library. We are going to see what we can learn about the solar system.

Sarah: Oh, I've always liked the planets. My Daddy shows me Jupiter and Mars sometimes when it isn't cloudy. What kinds of things will we be learning?

Mr. Holmes: Well, that depends on what you already know. Who can tell us something about the solar system?

Julie: The planets go around the sun!

Geoff: Jupiter is the biggest planet and it's got stripes . . . and Saturn has pretty rings on it.

Atchley: And NASA sent some spaceships to Mars. I saw the pictures on TV. Remember when you could see that comet? Are comets planets, too?

Mr. Holmes: Well, it sounds like we know some facts about the solar system, but we also have some questions. Let's take a minute to write down what we know and what kinds of things we want to find out. Then we'll go to the library and see what we can learn. After you've had a chance to explore some of the information there, I want each group to build a computer database of the solar system.

Julie: What kinds of stuff do we put in the computer?

Mr. Holmes: You and your group mates will have to decide what is the most important information for each planet. Later we'll look at everybody's databases to see how they compare.

It's easy to see how this exercise could then lead into discussions of what distinguishes one planet from another, what are the most important features of solar system objects, whether the different planets could support life, etc. It would then be a short step to making posters or models, writing reports, or even making web pages that describe what had been learned about the solar system.

CD-ROMs

There are literally hundreds of CD-ROMs now available for school use. Many tutorial programs take advantage of the huge storage capacity of these silver disks to store full-color photographs or even short movie clips. Some of the more popular vendors include Davidson, Sunburst, and Scholastic. Each has catalogs with many titles covering a wide range of topics. For example, Davidson's *Wanna Be a Dino Finder* lets students "dig" for 50 fossils at six different sites. They not only learn science, but also build knowledge of math and social studies. Davidson's *Discover Astronomy, RedShift 2,* or *Solar System Explorer* might be among the resources the students in the previous vignette locate in the library. For more earthbound studies, take a look at Sunburst's *Learn about Dinosaurs*–or Animals, Insects, Plants, Human Body, etc. (Pay attention to what type of computer the software runs on. Sunburst has been in the business for a long time and still offers programs for the Apple II and DOS platforms.) The Learning Team offers *Small Blue Planet,* which uses beautiful graphics to display deserts, mountains, and oceans. Students can even see a global map showing exactly where the sun is shining at that moment or at any time during the year.

For teachers wanting to put together science classes, it would be hard to find a CD-ROM more useful than Learning Team's *Science Helper K–8.* This single disk has 919 lesson plans incorporated into a database indexed by grade level, subject, process skill, keyword, and content. It includes materials developed for COPES, ESS, ESSP, MINNEMAST, SAPA, ACIS, and USMES.

Another interesting place to look for ideas is Al Bodzin's CD-ROM called *ISME: Instructional Materials for Science Education.* This disk is really a collection of material "harvested" from the Internet. (In fact, if you are trying to convince your administrators that useful material can be found on the web, this disk is the next best thing and might help your cause.)

Of course, don't forget the assortment of CD-ROM encyclopedias that are available. It is really amazing how much information will fit on one disk. There is a very nice comparison of these packages in the May/June '97 issue of *Electronic Learning.* The biggest sellers include Microsoft's *Encarta,* World Book's *Multimedia Encyclopedia,* Compton's *Interactive Encyclopedia,* and Grolier's *Multimedia Encyclopedia.*

Finally, the entire collection of 108 Years of *National Geographic* on 30 CDs is available for less than $200. There is a powerful search engine for topics, dates, titles, and issue. Every single copy is included—all the stories and every marvelous photograph. Talk about a learning resource!

Videodiscs

Optical Data's *Windows on Science* series (Primary, Life, Physical, and Earth Sciences) offers an entire science curriculum, including videodiscs with English/Spanish narrations, unit guides, image indexes, and sometimes CD-ROMs. Their *Insights* collection helps kids get going with inquiry-based learning. They also offer a *Minorities in Science* package that features four contemporary minority scientists and a database of hundreds more who have agreed to act as mentors to kids. They've got data from studies illustrating the sizable impact of their materials on learning. Offering special deals for schools, they are a good source of videodisc players and monitors. They even have a teacher training program, *Ms. Lerner,* that shows you how to best utilize videodiscs in the classroom. Videodiscovery has a large number of titles, including *Science Sleuths Elementary, Bio Sci Elementary,* and CDs on other subjects of interest to children.

Microcomputer-Based Labs (MBL)

Robert Tinker, one of the pioneers of microcomputer-based labs, is the director of the Concord Consortium, an organization which offers a wide variety of innovative instructional technology. Students can use Apple Computer's eMate (a portable classroom computer that can survive a 10-foot drop) to collect data during science experiments. Concord Consortium materials get students learning about rainforests through studies of local humidity and light. They also offer on-line discussion groups, experts that are only an e-mail note away, and ways to post and review data from around the world.

Another inexpensive way to get students collecting and analyzing data is with the calculator-based ranger (CBR) from Texas Instruments. This simple device plugs into a calculator and lets students see graphs of position or velocity as they walk around in front of the unit. Research has shown this type of activity to be highly effective. (See the Brasell article in the references for details.) Texas Instruments and Casio manufacture a wide variety of sensors which can plug into particular models of their calculators. These battery powered CBL (for calculator-based lab) units can be taken anywhere students want to sample data. Let's say you were teaching a series of lessons on the ecosystem of a stream and you have just talked about how fish "breathe" the oxygen that's dissolved in the water.

Mary: Ms. Zimmer, how does the oxygen get into the water for the fish?

Ms. Zimmer: Hmmm . . . that's a very good question. Does anybody have any ideas about how that might happen?

Billy: I've got an aquarium at home and I have to run a little pump that makes bubbles or the fish will die.

Joey: But there's no pump in the creek behind the playground and I seen fish in there! [Laughter]

Ms. Zimmer: "I *saw* fish," Joey. You're right, of course. But I *do* remember seeing bubbles in the water.

Mary: There's that little waterfall where there's lots of swirly water and all kinds of bubbles. Is that how the air gets in there?

Ms. Zimmer: Well, how would we find out?

Michele: Can we measure the air in the water somehow?

Ms. Zimmer: Our CBL can measure dissolved oxygen. We should be able to use that. While we're there, why don't we also use it to see if there has been any acid rain running into the stream.

Billy: When we're done with it, can I take it home and see how much air there is in my aquarium?

Being able to make measurements of things around them really helps kids see the relationship between science and the everyday world. And because these new sensors are so rugged, Ms. Zimmer might even let Billy take a CBL unit home for the night!

Other Materials

Some packages combine many different subject areas. *Investigating Lake Iluka* from The Learning Team helps students with biology, geography, and ecology through the use of a built in "notebook." It uses video, graphics, and sound to simulate the lake environment. Students investigate the ecosystem via physical, chemical, and biological measurements. *Culture and Technology,* from the same company, integrates social studies and science. There are 1,300 lessons that incorporate video, audio, and photos.

Creative Wonders offers *Wide World of Animals* and *Science Rock.* Features include curriculum integration strategies, correlations to regional and national standards, activity and lesson plans, blackline masters, and indexes of additional resources.

Two particularly interesting curriculum packages are the two *Voyage of the Mimi* material sets. Although they are mostly aimed at middle school children, you may find some appropriate for younger students. There are 12 or 13 videos (15 minute episodes + 15 minute documentaries, with real scientists and the episode actors stepping out of their roles to interview them). There are many role models and lots of applications of science to the real world all folded together into a series of exciting adventures. The comprehensive package also includes student booklets, activities, software, etc. If you are having a hard time getting your students involved in science, this is the way to go!

USING THE WORLD WIDE WEB

Sites for Teachers

As you are probably aware, there has been a major push to get schools connected to the Internet. The Federal Communication Commission set up the Universal Service Fund with money from telecom company surcharges. Its purpose is to provide virtually all elementary and secondary schools (public and private) with cut-rate web access. The fund covers hubs, routers, switches, wiring, and telcom services. For more information, check out www.jdltech.com. If you (or your administrators or PTA) are concerned about children finding inappropriate materials on the web, take a look at some of the filtering software that is available. A nice one for newsgroups is *Newstand* from Imagina. You can specify exactly what newsgroups you want to have available, and even have different sets available for different classes.

If you'd like to see what other schools are doing, visit Oak View Elementary's site at oakview.fcps.edu. If you are looking for schools your students can communicate with, try the International WWW Schools Registry at web66.coled.umn.edu/schools.html.

There are many web-sites dedicated to helping teachers. For on-line workshops, find kendaco.telbyte.com/billband/Presentation. html. SuperKids (www.superkids.com) has reviews of educational software. See if you can find the review of *Bill Nye the Science Guy: Stop the Rock* from Pacific International. Sunburst's Web Pack collections have up to 50 sites, clip art, backgrounds, and curricular-related activities. Lessons use open-ended, exploratory, creative, and factual approaches to learning, including lessons on the rainforest, astronomy, and the oceans. Also available are six lessons to guide third through twelfth graders on the use of the Internet.

The National Science Teachers' Associations *NSTA Reports!* often has articles on incorporating the web into the science classroom and usually has long lists of interesting web-sites to visit. Scholastic Network contains curriculum correlated to national standards, connections to scientists and other classrooms, search tools, and a large directory of teacher-reviewed web-sites. They also offer Scientists Online where teachers and students can ask real scientists questions about astronomy, meteorology, body, animals, dinosaurs, and other science topics. It is located at http://scholasticnetwork.com. You should also try to get familiar with the web search engines (usually just a single button click away for most browsers). See if you can locate the National Science Education Standards.

The Global Schoolhouse, http://www.gsh.org, offers all kinds of resources, including a place for your school to publish web pages for free. They also have on-line discussion forums, lesson plans, and a whole collection of links to other schools. The American School Directory offers web pages describing every single elementary, middle, and high school in the country. They are accessible by linking to http://www.aad.net.

The Annenberg/CPB Math and Science Project, the Harvard-Smithsonian Center for Astrophysics, and the Massachusetts Corporation for Educational Telecommunications have created *The Channel*. This is a combination of free satellite broadcasting service (check with your school district office or a nearby university for a download site) and web pages that delivers workshops and credit-bearing professional development classes to K–12 math and science teachers. Call 800-556-4376 or http://www.learner.org/k12/acpbtv for more information.

If you'd like to start with a more familiar medium, pick up a copy of *A Guide to Educational Resources on the Internet.* This 300-page book is loaded with projects, tips on designing learning environments, assistance in using e-mail, listservs and newsgroups, and searching tips. It was written by Cynthia Leshin, and is available from Allyn and Bacon for about $25.

Kid's Sites

There are thousands of interesting web pages for children to visit. The Concord Consortium offers something called NetAdventure which posts challenges in math, science, and technology every week-day. There are discussion groups, on-line experts, and as noted earlier, places to post and review data and evaluate joint results.

The JASON project at http://www.jasonproject.org has nearly a dozen different expeditions to the world's oceans, Iceland, Yellowstone, etc. This project, founded by Dr. Robert Sallard, is one of the more famous examples of kids collaborating over the net.

The Why Files are at http://whyfiles.news.wisc.edu. Twice-monthly updates bring students the science behind the news. This site is very nicely set up and easy for kids to use. (Although you'll probably find that your students generally have much less trouble using the Internet than you!)

NASA offers a rich collection of resources for teachers and students. Resources, projects, ideas and applications for teaching with the Internet are at http://quest.arc.nasa.gov/OER/EDRC22.html. There is also a videotape called "Global Quest II" that is available by calling 216-774-1051, ext 293. See if you can search their site and locate images from the Hubble Space Telescope or the latest Mars mission.

You can probably see that we could just continue listing site after site after site. But it is more important for you to learn for yourself how to locate things you need from the web. After checking http://nationalgeographic.com/kids,   http://www.nwf.org/kids (the National Wildlife Federation), and http://www.wwf.org (the World Wildlife Fund), see what else you and your students can find. Happy hunting!

DELTA PRINCIPLE PERSPECTIVE

The Internet was begun by a group of physicists who wanted to be able to share data. It is not hard to see that we are definitely beyond this strictly scholastic application of the web and are now well into Level II. The use of "web crawling" software that generates indexes for the search was certainly beyond the initial thoughts of the original designers of the web. We have rapidly gotten to the point where many businesses depend on web technology for their everyday operations. It's getting hard to find a large company that doesn't have its own web-site. You might ask your students to be on the lookout for web addresses in advertisements. They are getting more and more common. Although most schools aren't quite where they'd like to be in terms of Internet access, that will probably change soon. Because technology "updates" happen so rapidly, it's hard to imagine how we might be using it in the future. But it is clear that as Internet access gets to be even more commonplace and hardware/software capabilities continue to expand, there will be fundamental changes in how people relate to each other and to the world around them. If we want to offer the best instruction to our students, it's up to us to take full advantage of all the opportunities available.

THINK ABOUT

- How would you respond to a parent who doesn't want to allow their child to access the Internet?

- Is it possible to purchase a book that is completely up-to-date on technology and the Internet?

- Can you think of a situation where students could collect data using MBL probes, analyze that data with a spreadsheet, upload their findings to the Internet, and then compare their results with those of other students around the country? Are there particular types of studies where this is especially effective? Are there types of studies where it is not?

- If you had to choose between purchasing a CD-ROM drive for your library or having Internet access, which would you pick? Why?

- Is it better to have Internet access in the classroom, in the library, or in a computer lab? Justify your decision. What would be the advantages and disadvantages of each situation?

- A student asks to borrow a calculator and CBR unit to try "an experiment" at home. Would you let them? What factors would you consider in your decision?

- Your principal wants you to have your students use technology to gather and analyze data. Would you ask for a single computer with powerful software and probes or instead ask to spend the same amount of money on a box full of calculators with similar probes but much less powerful software?

SELECTED REFERENCES

Brasell, H. (1987). "The effect of real-time laboratory graphing on learning graphic representations of distance and velocity." *Journal of Research in Science Teaching,* 24, 385–395.

Glynn, S., and R. Duit. (1995). *Learning science in the schools: Research reforming practice.* Lawrence Erlbaum: Mahwa, NJ.

Renehan, Edward (1996). *Science on the web.* Springer-Verlag: New York. This book is an annotated list of more than 500 of the best science sites on the Internet.

Serim, Ferdi, and Melissa Koch (1996). *NetLearning: Why teachers use the Internet.* Songline Studios: Sebastopol, CA. This is a great book that gives lots of ideas for student-student and teacher-teacher collaborations.

Electronic Learning magazine is a good source of the latest information on this subject. Information is available at 800-554-2917. $24 per year subscription price.

You may want to look at the National Science Foundation's *Review of Instructional Materials for Middle School Science,* NSF 97-54, which is available at their website, http://www.nsf.gov.

Some useful contact information:

Concord Consortium
    http://www.concord.org

Creative Wonders,
    http://www.cwonders.com

Davidson Software, 800-545-7677,
    http://www.davd.com

Imagina, 800-909-6537,
  www.imagina.com

Learning Team, 800-793-TEAM

Optical Data, 800-201-7103,
  http://www.opticaldata.com

Scholastic, 800-SCHOLASTIC,
  http://www.scholastic.com

Sunburst, (800) 321-7511,
  http://www.sunburst.com

Videodiscovery, 800-548-3472,
  http://www.videodiscovery.com

Instructional Materials for Science Education CD-ROM is available from North Carolina State University's SERVIT Group,
  http://www2.ncsu.edu/unity/lockers/project/cepwebpt2/mathsci/imse/index.html

Texas Instruments Calculator-Based Ranger (CBR) plugs into TI-92, 83, 85, 86, 92 calculator and senses position for less than $100. 1-800-TI-CARES or ti-cares@ti.com

8 Enhancing Math Teaching with Technology

LOOKING AHEAD

Sharon phoned her parents to get advice about obtaining a mortgage for her first home. "Dad, what do I need to know?" she asked. Her father informed her about getting the best interest rate, about the fact that her monthly payments would include taxes and insurance, and about the closing costs that he remembered paying on his own mortgage years ago. When Sharon began to talk with bankers she was faced with a dizzying array of choices that were unheard of to her parents. Not only did she have to be concerned about the things her father was concerned about, but now she had choices about variable interest rates, balloon mortgages, convertible mortgages, private mortgage insurance, and on and on. To make matters worse, every lender had its own way of packaging the product so that comparison from lender to lender was nearly impossible. She soon realized that she needed to know how much this loan was going to cost her "up front" as well as how much it was going to cost her over time. If she could find a way to compute and compare these costs, then she could make an informed choice. After setting up a spreadsheet to handle the necessary computations, Sharon began to enter data and compare mortgages. Much to her surprise there was no clear winner: one mortgage was cheaper to obtain, but after five years it began costing more than any others. Another was more costly at first, but after seven years its overall costs were less, and so on. So, the spreadsheet couldn't make Sharon's decision for her, but at least now she knew another question that she had to take into consideration: How long would she be staying in this new house?

As educators we need to be concerned about preparing the "Sharons" of today's world mathematically. The mathematical challenges that they face are different than they have been at any time in history. The tools they will use to do mathematics are also different. Our school curriculum needs to make the most of the tools that are available. We need to be realistic about the world we are preparing our students for.

CAN YOU?

- Explain the difference between using a spreadsheet for modeling and using a spreadsheet for straight calculations?

- Design a spreadsheet that would be appropriate for use in grades 1 or 2?

- Define a spreadsheet construction task that would be appropriate for middle school students?

- Distinguish between controversial and non-controversial uses of the Logo programming language?

- Tell three principles to follow when using Logo to teach children about variables?

- Describe how the *Jasper* videodisc series might be used to help children learn mathematics?

- Identify some sites on the World Wide Web where resources for teaching mathematics are found?

- Explain why the World Wide Web is less suitable for mathematics projects than it is for projects in other areas of the curriculum?

TEACHER LABORATORY

Spend some time working with the Logo programming language. Learn how to make procedures that make shapes. Learn how to use procedures that you've written as commands in higher-level procedures. Make a recursive procedure. Make procedures that use variables.

Visit the Jasper Woodbury site on the World Wide Web (http://www.opticaldata.com/catalog/jasp-hom.htm) and see what you can find out about this innovative mathematics education technology.

USING THE TOOLS

A spreadsheet is far more than a tool for performing computations; it can be used for problem solving, modeling, and exploring. Used properly, with an emphasis on mathematical modeling and the visual display of computational processes, the spreadsheet can be a tool that helps children gain a deeper number sense. Clements (1989) emphasizes that "work with spreadsheets should involve such high-level activities as making and testing hypotheses and predictions, investigating the effects of changing one value on other values in the spreadsheet, exploring number patterns, and modeling complex situations." (p. 70). Hunt (1995) describes his own use of spreadsheets to create models of mathematical processes and his subsequent discovery that the creation of such models *by his students* was an important learning experience for them. We should use spreadsheets in these ways at all grade levels. We should provide prepared spreadsheets that make it possible for students to explore and discover relationships between numbers and formulas, but we should also provide students with the challenge of building their own spreadsheets for modeling and exploration.

In the primary grades a common mathematical activity that can be enhanced by the spreadsheet is skip-counting. With skip-counting, children are given a number and that becomes the starting number in a counting sequence. The counting sequence consists of "counting by" the increment of the starting number. Usually this is done orally, with children taking turns saying the next number in the counting sequence.

Skip-counting on the spreadsheet allows children to see patterns and explore numbers in a way that mere oral skip-counting cannot do. In this instance it is probably best to provide children with a prepared spreadsheet like the one in Figure 8–1.* In this

---

*The skip-counting example spreadsheet makes use of an absolute reference in the formula. Although it may be possible to teach the concept of absolute references to primary grade children, our emphasis here is on the children's exploration of numbers rather than on their learning of spreadsheet programming.

Skip Counting by $\boxed{9}$'s

Starting Number:	9
2nd number:	18
3rd number:	27
4th number:	36
5th number:	45
6th number:	54
7th number:	63
8th number:	72
9th number:	81
10th number:	90
11th number:	99
12th number:	108
13th number:	117
14th number:	126
15th number:	135
16th number:	144
17th number:	153
18th number:	162
19th number:	171
20th number:	180

Figure 8–1.   Skip-Counting Spreadsheet
The user enters the starting number in cell C2. Cell F2 contains the formula =C2.
Cells F3, F4, and so on contain the formula =F2+$C$2, =F3+$C$2, and so on.
The use of the $ in the formula makes cell C2 an absolute reference. The use of
a formula that refers to the output of a previous formula is an example of
recursion. The syntax and punctuation are correct for Microsoft Excel™.

spreadsheet the child enters a number in the box, and the spreadsheet produces the first twenty numbers in the counting sequence.
When the children do oral skip-counting, the intellectual challenge
for them is to think of the next number. When they use the spreadsheet for skip-counting, the intellectual challenge is different. The
teacher must pose interesting questions for the children, and the
children should be encouraged to pose interesting questions of their
own. The following set of questions can lead to some interesting explorations by the children:

Try skip-counting by all the numbers between 2 and 10.
Which skip-counts have no odd numbers in their lists? Why
do these skip-counts have no odd numbers? What do you
notice about these skip-count numbers? Which skip-counts
do you think will have no even numbers in their lists? Try

these numbers to see if you were right. Can you explain what happened and why it happened?

Children who have learned to enjoy such explorations often surprise their teachers by the observations they make about numbers. The following are some observations about numbers that children might make when they can examine and explore numbers using the skip-counting spreadsheet.

When you skip-count by 2s, the ones place numbers follow a pattern: 2,4,6,8,0, 2,4,6,8,0.

When you skip-count by 9s, the ones place numbers count down (9,8,7,6,5,4,3,2,1,0) and the tens place numbers count up (0,1,2,3,4,5,6,7,8,9).

When you skip-count by 5s, there are patterns too. The ones place goes 5,0,5,0 and the tens place goes 1,1,2,2,3,3,4,4 and so on.

When you skip-count by 3s, if you add the digits, there's always a pattern of 3, 6, 9.

Explorations of such characteristics of numbers are not trivial. Children who are comfortable making such observations are demonstrating a highly desirable attitude toward mathematics. They are also building a foundation for later understanding of multiplication facts and divisibility rules. Perhaps most important, they are developing an ability to pose their own questions and to find out that they can enjoy answering their own questions.

We do not suggest that spreadsheet explorations of skip-counting should replace oral skip-counting. There are great benefits to children that come from oral skip-counting. However, there are other great benefits to children that come from exploring skip-counting on a spreadsheet. Both types of activities will be seen in the best elementary classrooms.

In elementary classrooms, whole number arithmetic still occupies a large part of the mathematics curriculum. Instead of spending the majority of time on having students gain flawless pencil-and-paper proficiency, however, today's teachers are focusing more on helping children invent and understand algorithms. Spreadsheet modeling can be very helpful in this regard. Figure 8–2 presents a spreadsheet that was designed to model the algorithm for 2-digit by 2-digit multiplication. The student enters two 2-digit numbers, and

---

A MULTIPLICATION MACHINE

Enter a two-digit number in this box: | 56 |

Enter another two-digit number: × | 11 |

616

The Distributive Property

*56 = 50 + 6

× 11 = 10 + 1

Multiply ones by ones   1 × 6 = 6

Multiply ones by tens   1 × 50 = 50

Multiply tens by ones   10 × 6 = 60

Multiply tens by tens   10 × 50 = 500

Add   616

Figure 8–2.   A Multiplication-Algorithm Spreadsheet
With the exception of applying the distributive property, this spreadsheet uses simple multiplication and addition of various cells. The distributive property is applied by using the RIGHT and LEFT functions. The "5" at the * is obtained by applying the function =LEFT(6). The first 2-digit number entered by the student is in cell D6. In this manner the two 2-digit numbers entered by the student are separated into their tens and ones components. (This feature makes this spreadsheet unsuitable for multiplication of anything but 2-digits by 2-digits. A good task for students may be to modify this spreadsheet to work with other types of multiplication.)

the spreadsheet displays the product. More significantly, the spreadsheet applies the distributive property and shows the expanded form of the partial products and the numbers that were used to obtain them.

This spreadsheet is somewhat useful for students who are learning the standard multiplication algorithm. It provides a visual and dynamic display that shows where each partial product comes from and what it really means. As is true of most spreadsheets, students can enter a variety of input numbers and observe the effects on various parts of the expanded algorithm. It is probable that some students will be able to learn the standard multiplication algorithm by interacting with this spreadsheet model.

The greatest benefit of such a spreadsheet, however, is in the construction of it. Students may be shown the spreadsheet, and they should be permitted to use it and examine it fully. But ultimately they should be given the task of constructing an original algorithm-modeling spreadsheet of their own. As Hunt (1995) noted, ". . . one cannot program the spreadsheet to perform [algorithms], . . . unless a thorough understanding of the algorithms is already in place" (p. 774). Given the task of constructing a spreadsheet that "reveals" the multiplication algorithm, students will gain a deep understanding of that algorithm. Naturally, there will be a need to teach some features of spreadsheet programming, but these features will be learned in the service of a significant mathematical project.

Another helpful feature of spreadsheets is their ability to provide graphical representations of data. Many times children in the primary grades are asked to count and chart such things as how many children are wearing red today, how many children own a pet, what is your favorite ice cream, how many brothers do you have, and so on. Typically the primary grade teacher uses these counting exercises to develop a deeper understanding of numbers and their presence in our lives. Often the teacher takes the data that are collected in this way and turns them into a simple graph. The goal is to introduce children to graphical representation of data and to the beginning skills in reading graphical data. The spreadsheet can help the teacher with these tasks, and it can make it possible for children to start making their own graphs at a younger age than would be possible without the spreadsheet.

Without a spreadsheet, younger children are dependent on the teacher to make properly proportioned graphs. With the spreadsheet, these young children can make their own graphs. Without a spreadsheet, older children can make their own graphs, but it is a demanding and time-consuming task to make them correctly. With a spreadsheet, older children can make graphs quickly and easily, and they can devote their energies to higher-level thinking in relation to the data on the graphs. They can become involved in critical thinking exercises related to interpreting the graphs. Since the graphs change dynamically with the numbers in the spreadsheets, some children will prefer to use graphic representation of data as a tool to help them interpret the data.

The ability of spreadsheets to produce dynamic graphical representations of data also makes it possible for children to explore graphical models of functions. When children can see symbolic representations and graphical representations of functions as connected,

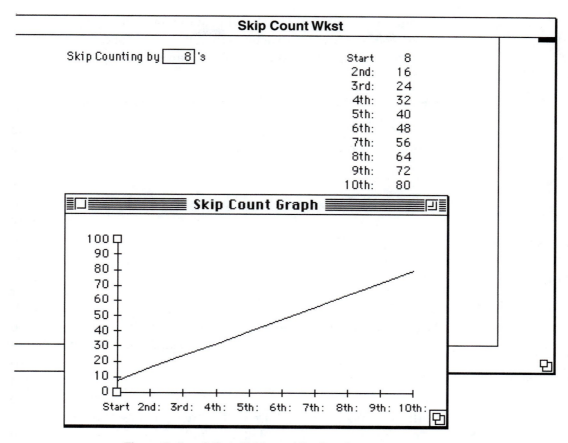

Figure 8–3.   A Data Table and Its Graph

they have made a major advance in their understanding of mathematics. The following vignette illustrates a group of children who are building these connections.

Mr. Ericson's fourth grade had been working on their multiplication tables. In order to help them deepen their understanding of multiplication as a function, he had modified the skip-counting spreadsheet that the children had used years earlier. He set up the spreadsheet so that it would provide a line graph of the first ten numbers in the skip-counting list. He had used the scaling options to force the vertical axis of the graph to be numbered from 0 to 100 in increments of ten. He had arranged the screen so that both the spreadsheet and the graph would be showing at the same time. In a learning center, he had instructions for children to follow in order to begin their explorations. Paul and Sarong were at the learning center.

Paul: OK, it says to start with skip-counting by 10s. Let's see what happens.

Sarong: Whoa! Look—it makes a line.

Paul: It's like a ramp or something.

Sarong: Now, it says to try skip-counting by 1s next. That's not really skip-counting.

Paul: Let's see what it does.

Sarong: It's low.

Paul: It's still a little bit of a ramp.

Paul: Next it says, "What do you think will happen with skip-counting by 5s?" I'll bet it will be a ramp that's steeper than 1 but not as steep as 10.

Sarong: Yeah, half-way. Let's see it. Yeah. We were right.

Paul: OK, now it says, "Try a lot more numbers. Write down any discoveries you make." Let's try 100.

Sarong: Hey! Nothing happens! There's no line!

Paul: Weird! Let's try 50.

Sarong: Look, it's a steep ramp, but it *starts* at the 50 and goes up. Hey, I didn't notice where the other lines were starting, did you?

Paul: No, let's do 10 again and see. Hey look, it starts at the 10!

Sarong: So, we can write down that the ramp starts at the number you put in.

Paul: Well sure; look: when we start skip-counting, our first number is the number we're counting by.

Sarong: Oh, man are we stupid. That's why there wasn't a line for 100! It *starts* at 100 and goes up.

USING EDUCATIONAL SOFTWARE

Logo

Since the early 1980s, the Logo programming language has been widely available as an educational tool. This programming language for children was designed at MIT under the direction of Seymour Papert. From its earliest versions, Logo was designed with child development considerations in mind. Although many versions of Logo have been written, and Logo continues to evolve, the feature that has been common to all versions since 1980 is turtle graphics. With turtle graphics a small triangle, or a small turtle-shaped object, moves around on the screen in response to commands typed by the user. As the turtle moves it leaves a line. By commanding the turtle through movements of FORWARD and BACK, and through turns of RIGHT and LEFT, children can create on-screen drawings and designs. Each of these commands also requires an input number: a number of "turtle steps" for FORWARD and BACK, and a number of degrees for turning RIGHT and LEFT. Users can control the turtle one command at a time, or they can write a series of commands into a "procedure" which can be executed by using the name of the procedure. Named procedures can then be used as command lines in higher-level procedures. This process of naming and using procedures allows the user to build the turtle's vocabulary.

Papert (1980) has had Delta Level III effects on learning as his goal from the beginning. Papert spent time in Geneva with noted researcher Jean Piaget, where he learned about children's cognitive development. He intended Logo as a tool for thinking which would allow children to become abstract thinkers at an earlier age than would otherwise be possible. Papert's vision has engendered a fascinating dichotomy of responses among educators. Many have become devoted Logo advocates and some have made impassioned claims about Logo's effectiveness as an educational tool. Others have expressed great criticism and skepticism about Logo's effects (Maddux, 1989).

One area of controversy has been in the area of problem solving. Advocates have claimed that children who learn to program computers using Logo have become better at *general* problem solving.

(See Roblyer, Castine, and King, 1988, for example.) Others have cited research that fails to support this claim. (See Pea and Kurland, 1984, for example.) It appears that the value of teaching programming with the hope that it will transfer into a general problem-solving skill is at least questionable.

A less-controversial area has been the use of Logo-based activities to teach children mathematics. Much research has been conducted to examine the effects of Logo on children's learning of geometry. Evidence has accumulated over time (Clements, Battista, Sarama, Swaminathan, and McMillen, 1997; Clements and Battista, 1989; Clements and Battista, 1990; Edwards, 1991) to indicate that carefully prepared materials that incorporate off-computer tasks, on-computer tasks, and geometric problem solving have a beneficial effect on children's learning of geometry (Clements, Nastasi, and Swaminathan, 1993). Apparently the effectiveness of Logo in geometry learning is due to the fact that Logo causes children to attend to properties of the shapes they are constructing. Tasks and activities that cause the children to focus on the procedural commands as they relate to spatial designs seem to help children advance to higher levels of geometric thinking (Riedesel, Schwartz, and Clements, 1996).

An example of the kind of activity that is beneficial is one where students are to figure out missing measurements on a Logo-drawn figure (see Figure 8–4). Tasks such as this one are used to help children begin to think of figures as being made from paths. Children who can perceive of geometric figures as being composed of sides

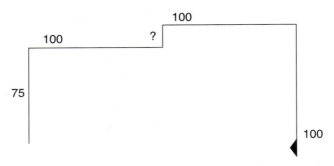

How long is the "?" piece?
How far will the turtle have to go to get back home?

Figure 8–4.   Logo Missing Measurements Task

and angles are at a higher level of geometric thinking than are children who perceive of geometric figures as whole objects.

Logo has also been suggested as a tool for helping young children construct a foundation for algebraic thinking. In particular, children can begin to formalize their intuitive notions of variables and *functions* through the use of Logo. Logo permits children to experiment with variables and functions in an environment where these algebraic concepts are dynamic. Children who learn about variables in a static environment often mistakenly think of a variable as representing a *particular* number. Children using Logo are not immune from this misconception, but a skilled teacher can provide scaffolding to enable the child to discover that the variable can represent *any* of a range of numbers. The following vignette illustrates a teaching situation in which a skilled teacher leads a student from a limited view of variables to a more generalized view.

The Task: Write a Logo procedure that will draw a rectangle whose length is always 10 steps longer than its width.

Cheryl: How about this:

TO REC

MAKE :STEPSWIDE 10

FORWARD :STEPSWIDE

RIGHT 90

FORWARD 20

RIGHT 90

FORWARD :STEPSWIDE

RIGHT 90

FORWARD 20

RIGHT 90

END

Ms. Tripp: Explain to me what the turtle does when it follows these steps.

Cheryl: It finds out that :STEPSWIDE is 10, then every time it sees STEPSWIDE it knows that it's 10. So in the next line, when it sees FORWARD :STEPSWIDE it goes forward 10 steps. Then it turns and makes the next side 20, which is 10 more than the first side. Then it does FORWARD :STEPSWIDE again, then FOR-WARD 20 again.

Ms. Tripp: So, it makes a rectangle whose sides are 10 and 20? Is this what The Task asked for?

Cheryl: Well, I think so. The length is 10 more than the width.

Ms. Tripp: What if we wanted it to make rectangles of *different* sizes, but with a length always 10 more than the width? Do you remember that we can put a variable in the naming line of the procedure so that the procedure will take an input?

Cheryl: Oh, like this?

TO REC :STEPSWIDE

Ms. Tripp: Yes, now, will that work, or will you have to change other parts of your procedure?

Cheryl: It'll work if you tell it to REC 10.

Ms. Tripp: OK, but what if someone tells it to REC 15? or REC 57?

Cheryl: Hmmm. Let's try it. I don't think it will work.

She tries these inputs.

Cheryl: Nope. The length stays at 20. Can you put a bunch of different lengths in, just in case someone chooses REC 15 or REC 57? That seems pretty complicated.

Ms. Tripp: You're right. It should be simpler than that. Why don't you find a way to use STEPSWIDE? Doesn't STEPSWIDE hold whatever number the person types next to REC?

Cheryl: Yes. . . , and the length is supposed to be 10 more than that. Can I do math with it? Can I make it :STEPSWIDE + 10?

Ms. Tripp: Try that and see what happens. Try it with a lot of different inputs for REC.

In using Logo, children can have many opportunities to use variables to carry out actions. They can learn the foundations of algebra through actions that they tell the computer to carry out. The actions of the computer provide immediate feedback to the children to allow them to refine their thinking. There is a connection between a symbolic representation (the Logo procedure) and a visual representation. The use of actions to explore mathematical abstraction, the immediate feedback, and the connection between different types of representations all make Logo an ideal environment for learning mathematics. The focus here is on learning mathematics, rather than on learning programming. Students will certainly learn some important things about programming, but that is not the central goal.

Clements and Sarama (1997) cite several research studies that indicate that Logo can be effectively used to help children develop a better understanding of variables. They conclude that teachers should keep three principles in mind when using Logo to teach about variables. First, students should learn to identify what is varying (students have to examine a procedure to find all the instances where a particular variable is needed); second, the names they choose for variables should be descriptive of exactly what is varying; and third, students should use the variables with operations (like :length * .5, or :length + 5).

Jasper Series

One of the most exciting newer products that uses technology to enhance the teaching of mathematics is an optical laserdisc-based product known as the *Jasper Series.* Produced at Vanderbilt University's Peabody College of Education, and marketed by Optical Data Corporation, this 3-disc series presents dramatic video adventures that lead children into a problem-solving situation. The video adventures are under the control of a computer, and the accompanying software allows students to search the video and replay selected portions. It also provides background data that is needed for solving the problems. Typically the video adventure presents a context for a rich mathematical problem-solving investigation. In one episode an injured eagle is found in a remote area and a number of options are explored as methods of rescuing the eagle. Each of the options has difficulties, such as limited access for ground transportation, limited fuel/weight/range ratio for an ultra-light aircraft, and so on. The students must research the options, search for information (in the video and software data bank), compare benefits and drawbacks of each option, and eventually plan a solution to the problem. When their decision has been reached, the students enter their solution into the computer and the adventure continues on the basis of their choice of action. The *Jasper Series* is designed for upper elementary and middle school students.

The developers of the *Jasper Series* have described three ways in which these materials might be used in a classroom. One of these ways of using the materials would be to first teach children their basic mathematics skills and then bring in the Jasper materials to provide instruction in problem solving. This use of the materials would not be consistent with the philosophy around which the materials were designed. This use would represent Level I of the Delta Principle: a traditional understanding of teaching mathematics is assumed, where instruction in basic skills precedes instruction in problem solving, and the technology is used to strengthen this type of teaching.

A second way of using the Jasper materials would be for the teacher to provide highly structured worksheets and tasks to guide the children to problem solutions. This represents an instructional model that became popular in the 1980s in which problem-solving strategies became a focus of instruction. This use of the materials would still represent Level I in the Delta Principle; there is simply a different emphasis in the instruction. The Jasper materials might make this kind of teaching easier, but they are not being used to change teaching and learning significantly.

The third way of using the Jasper materials is quite different from the first two. In this case the teacher would provide some structure in the form of scaffolding early in the experience, but the goal would be to withdraw it, enabling the learners to function without it. This way of using the materials represents a constructivist philosophy, and this is the philosophy that the designers of the materials hold (Cognition and Technology Group at Vanderbilt, 1992). Under this model the goal is to provide the learners with some autonomy and an opportunity to try out their own ideas in a realistic context. Although these goals are not new, nor are they dependent on technology, they are sometimes difficult to achieve without the kinds of materials represented by the *Jasper Series*. This use of the Jasper materials might be characterized as being at Level III of the Delta Principle.

USING THE WORLD WIDE WEB

As a location for teaching resources, the World Wide Web supports mathematics education as well as it supports any other area of the curriculum. The National Council of Teachers of Mathematics maintains a web-site at http://www.nctm.org/. Here you can find information about the latest edition of the NCTM Standards, information about NCTM conferences, and various other NCTM services. Lesson plans, activities, and projects can be found at a number of sites, including one maintained by Houghton Mifflin at http://www.eduplace.com/math/index.html. A site called The Explorer (http://server2.greatlakes.k12.mi.us/) offers a searchable database system containing activities, lesson plans, and downloadable software for K–12 mathematics and science. "The Explorer is being developed jointly by the Great Lakes Collaborative and the University of Kansas UNITE group to involve educators and students in creating and using multimedia resources for active learning and 'on time' delivery. The U.S. Department of Education OERI office provided funding to support The Explorer research and development efforts". An excellent site that has links to many areas of interest is the site for Science and Math Initiatives (SAMI), which is maintained by the Annenburg CPB Foundation. Its location is http://www.learner.org/content/k12/sami/. A teacher in search of good ideas both for the classroom and for the school district can find much help at these locations.

However, the World Wide Web as a means of communication and as a site for student projects is less helpful in mathematics education than it is in other areas of the curriculum. There are sites, such as The Virtual School (http://www.webcom.com/~vschool/), where students can find mathematics problems to solve and to which they can submit their solutions in a sort of ongoing contest. This has some value because the operators of the site share interesting solution methods that have been submitted. One must choose web-sites carefully, however, to ensure that there is more value to students in communicating mathematics over the web than in communicating mathematics face-to-face in the classroom. Mathematics is an area in which live, face-to-face communication generally has more value than does the asynchronous form of communication that the web supports so well.

In order to justify the trade-off in mathematics education between the benefits of face-to-face communication and the inherent drawbacks (for mathematics) of asynchronous communication, there must be a compelling benefit to be achieved by using asynchronous communication. One such benefit would be to obtain mathematical measurements and perspectives from children in different parts of the world. KIDLINK IRC (http://www.kidlink.org/IRC/) can be helpful to children who are learning about different time zones in different parts of the world. Since children from all over the world participate in KIDLINK, the administrators of KIDLINK IRC have chosen Greenwich Mean Time (GMT) as the official time zone to use in posting requests for chat sessions. Children who want to participate in a chat or who want to initiate a chat must figure out how to convert their time into GMT. This is a wonderful way to give a real context to a mathematical problem. It is also an excellent way to integrate the teaching of mathematics and geography.

An example where children from various points on the earth's surface provide measurements is found in the Maya Math software which is part of the Bank Street College of Education's *Second Voyage of the MIMI* package. In this case, children are seeking to discover a relationship between latitude and the angle of the sun at solar noon. The children determine when solar noon occurs for them, and they measure the angle of the sun above the horizon at that point in the day. They then seek children from around the world to do the same thing at their locations. When the data are returned, the children make a number of diagrams to indicate the angle of the sun at the various locations around the earth. Again, the World Wide Web provides an opportunity for mathematics work in a global context. In this case the context is a scientific investigation, and integrated teaching of mathematics and science is supported.

DELTA PRINCIPLE PERSPECTIVE

How might the use of spreadsheets, Logo, programs like the *Jasper Series,* and creative use of the World Wide Web actually change the way children think mathematically? In the hands of a teacher who lacks the philosophical orientation found in the NCTM Standards (National Council of Teachers of Mathematics, 1989), these technologies will not cause change. As we illustrated in our discussion of the Jasper materials, the materials themselves can be used in ways that do not support change. However, in the hands of teachers who support the goals of the NCTM Standards, these technologies can provide very helpful leverage in bringing about meaningful change.

It is important to realize that the *existence* of calculators and computers has already changed one of the three primary forces* that drive curriculum: the needs of society. Because adults in our society no longer need to rely on pencil-and-paper algorithms to perform mathematical tasks, the curriculum of the schools is undergoing pressure to change. One of the underlying motivations for the writing of the NCTM Standards is an acknowledgment by mathematics educators that the need for pencil-and-paper arithmetic has diminished in our society.

Since we now rely heavily on electronic devices to do our arithmetic, we must focus our school curriculum on mathematical activities and tasks that only humans can do. This means that the majority of our time in mathematics classes should be spent on higher-level thinking, problem solving, and creative interpretations of data. The kinds of mathematical abilities that have become important might be termed "dynamic mathematics." Numbers are constantly changing; underlying relationships between the numbers become the object of study. The technologies that have been described in this chapter are ideal for stimulating the kinds of thinking that are needed in today's mathematics classrooms. The use of these technologies is an appropriate response to the changes in curriculum that are currently underway.

---

*According to Glennon and Callahan (1975), the curriculum of schools is determined by three competing needs: the needs of the child, the needs of society, and the needs of the subject (discipline).

Taken further, the use of these technologies can lead us to further changes. In the time before these technologies existed, only a relatively small handful of students completed four years of mathematics in high school. During those four years their mathematics instruction generally included algebra, geometry, trigonometry, and perhaps an introduction to calculus. These courses involved a good deal of computation in order for the conceptual foundations to become clear. Today, through the use of spreadsheets, Logo, problem solving software, and, in high school, graphing calculators, the conceptual foundations of the higher branches of mathematics can be made accessible to nearly everyone. Further, with a conceptual understanding, and a working knowledge of the basic electronic tools, nearly everyone should be able to apply these mathematics to everyday life. Instead of depending on a mathematical elite, tomorrow's citizens will be able to do their own mathematical thinking. This has profound political implications which are beyond the scope of this book.

Not only will more people be capable of mathematical thinking, but the kind of mathematical thinking they do will be profoundly different from the kind of mathematical thinking that was done by earlier generations. Without technology, the greatest value had to be placed on accuracy, precision, and speed in performing computational algorithms. With technology, the greatest value is placed on such abilities as evaluating reasonableness of answers, creating viable models, and determining the best questions to ask. Past generations had to have the ability to calculate how much of their paycheck would be withheld for social security. Today's generations are using their spreadsheets to determine the effects of compound interest on their retirement savings accounts. Again, the political implications of these changes are profound, and they are beyond the scope of this text.

The other side of the issue is that with less emphasis being placed on pencil-and-paper algorithms, tomorrow's children will be less skilled in this area than were earlier generations. Their speed and accuracy with pencil-and-paper computations will perhaps decline. If the effectiveness of our schools is judged solely by scores on tests that measure such skills, we could become convinced that our schools are failing in their effectiveness. Indeed, lower scores on such tests *can* indicate a decline in the effectiveness of our schools, if such declines are not offset by gains in the areas of thinking and problem solving. In order to accurately determine whether or not our schools are losing effectiveness, we must assess the new skills that the new, technology-driven curricula will be developing. One of the unfortunate effects of these curriculum and assessment changes is that proper assessment of these new skills is much more time-consuming and expensive than was assessment of pencil-and-paper arithmetic skills. Our communities must be willing to bear this greater expense of "authentic assessment." Unfortunately this comes at a time when any increases in spending of public money are viewed with great suspicion. So, in spite of the hope that technology will reduce the cost of basic education, it seems likely that the cost of education will be higher as a result of technology. This is certainly a negative effect of the changes.

THINK ABOUT

- If our schools teach children to use spreadsheets to model mathematics, must the schools also insist on flawless pencil-and-paper computation abilities?

- What are some further examples of mathematics tasks that children can engage in with spreadsheets that they could not engage in without spreadsheets?

- Evaluate the following statement: "Learning geometry through Logo activities is too costly in terms of time because children must first learn Logo before they can learn geometry."

- Should children in elementary school be expected to learn about variables and functions? Does your answer to this question *depend* on whether or not technology is used?

- What are the implications of teaching a mathematics curriculum that is dependent upon technology? What are the benefits of such a program? What are the dangers of such a program? Be very critical of your own answers here. Try to find some evidence upon which to build your thinking.

- When did technology begin to play an important role in the learning of mathematics? Be careful how you define "technology" here.

SELECTED REFERENCES

Clements, D. H. (1989). *Computers in elementary mathematics education.* Englewood Cliffs, NJ: Prentice Hall.

Clements, D. H., and Battista, M. T. (1989). "Learning of geometric concepts in a Logo environment." *Journal for Research in Mathematics Education, 20,* 450–467.

Clements, D. H., and Battista, M. T. (1990). "The effects of Logo on children's conceptualizations of angle and polygons." *Journal for Research in Mathematics Education, 21,* 356–371.

Clements, D., Battista, M., Sarama, J., Swaminathan, S., and McMillen, S. (1997). "Students' development of length concepts in a Logo-based unit on geometric paths." *Journal for Research in Mathematics Education, 28*(1), 70–95.

Clements, D. H., Nastasi, B. K., and Swaminathan, S. (1993). "Young children and computers: Crossroads and directions from research." *Young Children, 48,* 56–64.

Clements, D. H., and Sarama, J. (1997). "Computers support algebraic thinking." *Teaching Children Mathematics, 3*(6), 320–325.

Cognition and Technology Group at Vanderbilt (1992). "The Jasper experiment: An exploration of issues in learning and instructional design." *Educational Technology Research and Development, 40*(1), 65–80.

Edwards, L. D. (1991). "Children's learning in a computer microworld for transformation geometry." *Journal for Research in Mathematics Education, 22*(2), 122–137.

Glennon, V. J., and Callahan, L. C. (1975). *Elementary school mathematics: A guide to current research.* Washington, DC: Association for Supervision and Curriculum Development NEA.

Hunt, W. (1995). "Technology tips: Spreadsheets—a tool for the mathematics classroom." *Mathematics Teacher, 88*(9), 774–777.

Maddux, C. (1989). "Logo: Scientific dedication or religious fanaticism in the 1990s?" *Educational Technology,* February, 18–23.

National Council of Teachers of Mathematics (1989). *Curriculum and evaluation standards for school mathematics.* Reston, VA: National Council of Teachers of Mathematics.

Papert, S. (1980). *Mindstorms: Children, computers, and powerful ideas.* New York: Basic Books.

Pea, R. D., and Kurland, D. M. (1984). *Logo programming and the development of planning skills* (Technical Report No. 16). Bank Street College of Education, Center for Children and Technology.

Riedesel, C. A., Schwartz, J. E., and Clements, D. H. (1996). *Teaching elementary school mathematics* (6th ed.). Boston: Allyn and Bacon.

Roblyer, M. D., Castine, W. H., and King, F. J. (1988). *Assessing the impact of computer-based instruction: A review of recent research.* New York: Hawthorn Press.

9 Enhancing Reading and Language Arts Teaching with Computers

LOOKING AHEAD

Imagine a conversation between a new teacher and a retiring teacher in the year 1500. The time is shortly after the introduction of the printing press.

Jonathan: I don't envy you. You and your generation are going to have a devil of a time teaching the children of today. They're being ruined by this new machinery.

Gunther: I don't understand. What do you mean? I think this is the most exciting time in history to be teaching.

Jonathan: Well, with this new machine, the printing press, everyone is going to forget how to speak and how to listen. Instead of telling stories people will be writing them down. People will forget how to tell a story properly. Instead of listening to their lessons children will be reading them. No one will listen well any more. I tell you, I don't envy you.

Gunther: But think of it: When a story is written down you know it won't be changed every time someone tells it. The story becomes permanent when it's written down. We'll know that everyone is getting the exact same story.

Jonathan: But you can't tell me that written stories will be as good as spoken stories. How can you get emotions into writing? How can you get facial expressions into writing? How can you get body language into writing? I tell you, people are going to be in trouble.

Gunther: Well, when I read a story I imagine the emotions and the facial expressions and the body language. It probably isn't as good as listening to a good story, but these things aren't totally missing.

Jonathan: Well what about people's listening skills? I can see it now: Everyone will have to repeat everything they want people to hear because no one will know how to listen any more.

Gunther: You may have a point there. Listening won't be so important in the future. But, maybe that's an acceptable trade-off for the benefits of having everyone learn to read.

Jonathan: I tell you, I'm glad I'm retiring. I don't know what's becoming of the world these days.

Did you see some issues in this conversation that are parallel to the dialog today about using computers and communications technology in schools? Today's children have a need for skills that their parents never needed. At the same time there is a diminishing need for certain skills that were of great importance a generation ago. In hindsight we can see that the change from oral language to printed language was a valuable exchange. The benefits clearly outweighed the disadvantages. Will it be the same with the shift toward electronic forms of communication? Whether or not we believe it is the best direction to go, the world is experiencing a major shift in the way we handle communication. This chapter focuses on the technologies that are available today to help our children enter the world of electronic communication.

CAN YOU?

- Describe some ways in which word processing can help teach writing and reading?

- Debate both sides of the question of whether spell-check features of word processors are helpful or harmful to children?

- Identify some information-locating skills that today's students need?

- Describe how a database is useful for teaching today's information-locating skills?

- Tell how visual organizers and draw/paint tools may be used in the language arts curriculum?

- Identify some educational software titles that can be helpful in teaching reading and language arts?

- Describe some ways to find keypals for your students on the World Wide Web?

- Describe the value to children, in terms of language development, of using live on-line chats in the classroom?

TEACHER LABORATORY

Ask the following questions to high school graduates from 1995, 1985, 1975, and 1965. Do you read a newspaper daily? Do you watch television news daily? Do you regularly read books? Do you regularly use the World Wide Web to get information? Do you regularly use the World Wide Web for entertainment? Do you touch-type?

After conducting this informal survey, compare your findings with those of your classmates. Do you find any trends emerging from your data? Do you have any evidence that there are changes underway in terms of how people get information?

USING THE TOOLS

From the toolkit of word processing software, spreadsheets, databases, and drawing/painting tools, we can select two or three which are especially pertinent to the teaching of reading and language arts. Word processing has great potential for influencing the teaching of writing and reading. Database software is helpful for teaching information-locating skills. Draw/paint software can be included here because of its usefulness in helping children to communicate.

Word Processing for Teaching Writing

In recently reported research into first and second graders' reading and writing instruction, technology rich classrooms were compared to non-technology rich classrooms (Guthrie and Rosenzweig, 1997). The findings, as they related to student use of word processing, are interesting:

> Teachers consistently reported that their students wrote longer and more complex stories and put in more effort when using the computer. Students also seemed to spend more time developing and polishing their work, because editing was easier and because seeing their work printed out and illustrated provided a strong incentive.

Using word processing to help in the teaching of writing has some great advantages as well as some obstacles. The greatest benefits of word processing have to do with the fluidity of the writing that is encouraged by word processing. When writers generate their stories and reports with word processing, the words are so easily edited that it makes revision much more likely than it would be through pencil-and-paper writing. Language arts and writing teachers have long known that writing instruction should emphasize both the *process* of writing and the written *product*. With pencil-and-paper writing, it is very difficult for children to revise their work. But with word processing, revision is easy and natural; until a hard copy is printed the work has the character of a rough draft in process. Students are much more likely to engage in multiple revisions with word processing software to compose their work. Using word processing from the very earliest stages of teaching writing can help children learn the *process* of writing.

A second benefit to teaching writing through word processing is the benefit children obtain from using the spell-check feature of word processors. When children use the computer to check their spelling, one (obvious) result is that they can turn in work that is correctly spelled. While some would question whether spell-checkers are actually helpful to children in developing their own spelling skills, we maintain that having the computer point out incorrectly spelled words is somewhat akin to having a personal writing tutor working with the child as (s)he is working. Since the spell-checker does not *prevent* misspellings, and since the child must still respond to the suggestions of the spell-checker, the end result should be improved spelling skills. For example: If a child has repeated difficulty spelling a particular word, use of the spell-checker will provide repeated corrections. The repetition has the function of on-time, as-needed drill and practice. It is hard to imagine a more effective way to learn to spell correctly. Benefits, however, do not occur automatically. If children simply tell the computer to replace every flagged word with the first suggestion from the computer, they may not learn to become better spellers. Furthermore, their writing may contain some very strange words because the computer cannot suggest correct words based on meaning and context.

According to Anderson-Inman and Knox-Quinn (1996), teachers can encourage thoughtful and productive use of spell-checkers by teaching a few simple strategies for use with spell-check software. One such strategy addresses the problem that children have when the spell-checker suggests a number of alternatives to a flagged word and the writer does not know which of the alternatives is the intended word. (The spell-checker might suggest reveres, reverse, reveries, and reverts for the flagged misspelling *revers*.) In this case it is helpful if the writer has available an on-line dictionary. The strategy would be to use the on-line dictionary to look up each alternative until the word with the intended meaning is found. Another strategy is used when the spell-checker cannot find any alternative spellings for the misspelled word. (A spell-checker might be unable to suggest alternatives for *cumbustchen,* for example.) In this case the plan would be to systematically modify the misspelled word until the spell-checker is able to find an alternative. The first change should be a change to a vowel. (Try *combustchen.*) If the vowel changes fail, the next step would be to find alternative consonant combinations. (Try *combuschen.*) Using these strategies the writer can relatively quickly find the correct spelling for the unknown word. A third, and more complex, strategy is suggested for finding inappropriate uses of homophones. (For example, a spell-checker cannot distinguish between *principle* and *principal.*) In this case Anderson-Inman and Knox-Quinn (1996) suggest having available a document that lists common homophone pairs. Students would retrieve this document, select words from the list, and use the find feature to search for instances of those words in the paper under review. When they find instances of the homophone words, they can check in the on-line dictionary to see if the meaning of the found word is the intended meaning. Using these three strategies children can benefit greatly from the use of spell-checking features of word processing software.

The most obvious obstacle related to teaching writing through word processing is the fact that words must be entered by typing at the keyboard. Although there are predictions that the computer keyboard will become obsolete as a tool for entering text, up to now this has not occurred. In previous generations keyboarding skills were part of the high school curriculum, and they were not required of everyone. Today virtually everyone needs to learn keyboarding skills, and it is necessary to teach these skills in the elementary school. Land and Turner (1996) suggest that teachers can do this in a formal way beginning in grade four. Prior to grade four the major objectives for children include using the left hand for the left side of the keyboard and the right hand for the right side of the keyboard (grades 1 and 2), and using the home row of keys (grades 2 and 3).

A debatable issue surrounding the teaching of keyboarding is the question of whether or not children should engage in word processing before they have mastered keyboarding skills. If they do so, then there is a likelihood that they will develop "bad habits" in the use of their fingers on the keys. However, if they must wait until grade four to use word processing, they will miss out on the benefits of word processing in their earliest years. While both arguments have merit, it seems clear that the full benefits of word processing will not be available to children until they are proficient touch-typists. Some of the benefits of creating written communications electronically are available through authoring programs that are designed to minimize the need for typing. Programs such as *Imagination Express* (from Edmark Co.) allow children to *assemble* multimedia stories using a few words, but with lots of pictures and sounds that are supplied in the software. When young children use this type of software they can become authors of electronic works, including the vital act of revision, without being hindered by a lack of keyboarding skills. Another way in which word processing benefits can be made available to non-typists is to use software that converts speech input to written text. This is explored more fully in the next section.

Word Processing for Early Reading Instruction

One of the more promising technologies that can be used with word processing software in grades K–3 is a system that translates speech into text. Before they are proficient with the keyboard, children can speak into a computer microphone with the computer translating their spoken words into text. This activity in itself has tremendous value in helping children learn the connection between spoken language and written language. When children speak a sentence and then immediately "read" their own words, they learn quickly that written words represent spoken words. Teachers can give children tasks that draw their attention to the relationships between sounds and letters.

After children have "composed" prose using this system, they can then share with one another the material that they have "written." By reading one another's work they receive practice reading language at their appropriate developmental level.

Some teachers might be aware of a typical unintended negative outcome. If children can speak to their computer and have their computer put their words into writing, what will be the motivation for the children to learn the difficult task of writing by hand? This possible unintended negative outcome may be more of a fear that adults have rather than a real threat. The proposed diminished motivation for learning to write by hand may be more than offset by the fact that young children will be able to realize the purpose for learning to write much more readily than they would otherwise. If children are given many opportunities to enjoy the connection between speaking and writing and reading, it appears likely that they will quickly gain an understanding of the importance of learning to write. Children who lack these experiences may have more of a tendency to view writing instruction as drudgery and meaningless hard work.

Using Database Software to Teach Information-Locating Skills

Traditionally language arts instruction has included such objectives as using an index and a table of contents; using the card catalog; and using tools such as encyclopedias, dictionaries, and atlases. While these skills are important, a new collection of information-locating skills must be included in today's classroom. Since much of today's information is stored in electronic databases of various types, children must also learn to retrieve information from these sources.

Since there is a good deal of similarity among various electronic databases, it is possible to use one of them as an example of how to teach the generic skill of electronic searching. A good choice would be an electronic encyclopedia such as Microsoft's *Encarta*™*. Using a simple word search, a student might try to locate information on volcanoes (see Figure 9–1). Notice that even with a "simple" word search the student can make many selections as to the type of material to be

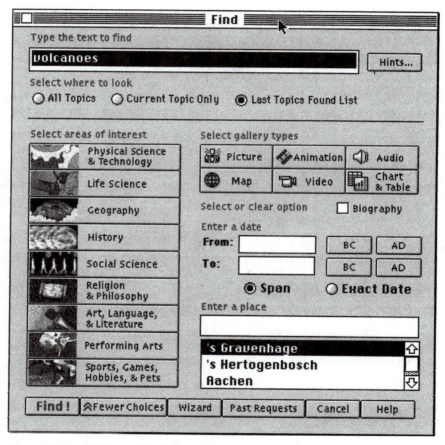

Figure 9–1. A Simple Word Search
Screen shot reprinted with permission from Microsoft Corporation.

*Microsoft Encarta is a trademark of the Microsoft Corporation.

found. This simple search turns up 177 places in the encyclopedia where the search term "volcanoes" is found. Since this is more hits than can reasonably be used, the student should refine the search with the AND operator. (S)he combines the terms "volcanoes" AND "Mount Saint Helens." The student discovers that even this narrower search does not yield a small enough number of hits. In this case the student wants to include only articles and materials related to Mount Saint Helens, so (s)he tells the encyclopedia to search for the name "Mt. St. Helens." Surprisingly, *no* articles or materials are found with this search term. Since there are alternative forms of abbreviation for this mountain's name, the student now needs to broaden the search using the OR operator. The new search will be as follows:

"Mount Saint Helens" OR "Mt. Saint Helens" OR "Mount St. Helens" OR "Mt. St. Helens"

This advanced search looks for entries that include the name of the particular mountain using *any* of the four variant abbreviations. This advanced search provides a reasonable number of hits: 12 (see Figure 9–2). One of these 12 is "Saint Helens, Mount" which is in a format that we had not thought of searching for. Clicking on this entry retrieves the encyclopedia's material for "Saint Helens, Mount." Since this is a typical student, (s)he begins by clicking on the camera in order to look at the photograph (see Figure 9–3). Finally, after looking at the photograph, the student returns to the text article about this volcano (see Figure 9–4). The skills demonstrated here represent the kind of information-locating skills that can reasonably only be taught by using the actual electronic database. These are the new skills needed by today's children.

Using Visual Organizers

Writers and teachers of writing have discovered the value of using webs as visual organizers to help with pre-writing activities. One of the problems with drawing webs on the chalkboard or on chart

Figure 9–2.   Advanced Search Results
Screen shot reprinted with permission from Microsoft Corporation.

paper is that it is difficult to revise a web once it is drawn. This is particularly problematic given the fact that the web is often used to record brainstorming sessions. It is difficult to plan how a web will look when the brainstorming is finished. The computer is the ideal place to create a web, and software companies have begun to produce software to enable this. One such software title is *Inspiration* from Inspiration Software. This software allows a writer to create a web directly on the computer screen. Optionally, one can create an outline first and have the software convert the outline to a web. It is even possible to toggle back and forth between the web and the outline. The software allows the web-maker to edit and move bubbles in order to create room for new thoughts. It allows for all bubbles at a given level of detail to share a common graphical form. This tool can be used by individual students or by the teacher using it with a computer screen projection device.

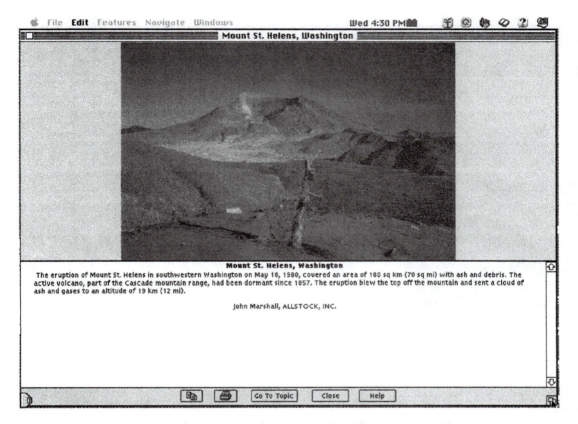

Figure 9–3.   A Photo Found Through the Advanced Search
Screen shot reprinted with permission from Microsoft Corporation.

Using Drawing/Painting Tools to Teach Graphic Communication

Creating computer graphics through the use of draw and paint programs has become an important part of written communication. Kidpix™, from Broderbund, is a software title that was developed in order to give children an appealing set of computer painting tools. There are a variety of tools that go beyond the traditional set of tools found in a paint program for adults. The special tools for Kidpix™ allow children to do such things as stamp appealing icons on their work, add sound effects, draw with a symmetrical mirror-image generated by the computer, and erase with a simulated explosion of

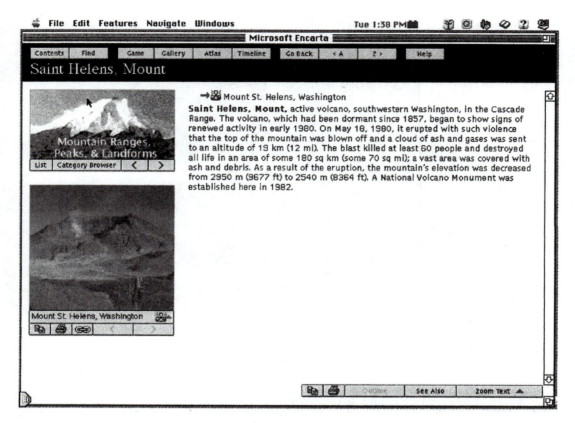

Figure 9–4.   A Text Article Found through the Advanced Search
Screen shot reprinted with permission from Microsoft Corporation.

dynamite. Teachers have found that children enjoy using the Kid-pix™ software to enhance their written work. Some typical uses of Kidpix™ are as follows: illustrating stories, creating greeting cards, creating picture-journals, illustrating invitations to special class events, writing rebus stories, and creating graphic representations of self. Since the tools are so easy and fun to use, the children generally produce much more creative work than their teachers anticipate. Working with Kidpix™ is a good training ground for the kind of visual communication these children will be doing all their lives. It enables them to experiment with color, form, design, and balance as they try to express themselves visually.

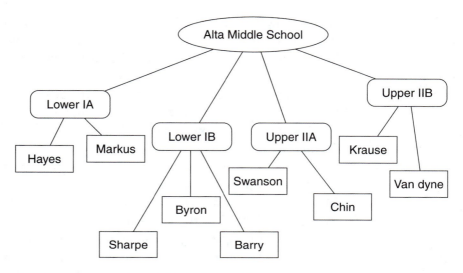

Figure 9–5. A Web as a Visual Organizer

Programs like KidPix™ and ClarisWorks™, while they are useful for teaching language and reading skills, were not designed specifically for classroom use. In this sense their use in education might be said to be a Delta Level II use of this type of software. In contrast to this there is software that has been specifically designed for teaching reading and language arts. Representative titles of this type of software are examined in the next section.

USING EDUCATIONAL SOFTWARE

One type of educational software that is related to the teaching of reading and language arts is children's books on CD. One of the earliest companies to develop this type of software was Discis Books. One of the products of Discis Books was Aesop's Fables on CD. The CD version of the book offered many features that are of interest to reading teachers. The computer presented a book-like interface on the screen. There were two pages showing, one of which had illustrations and the other of which had words. Some of the words were highlighted, and when these words were clicked a computer voice pronounced them. Children could opt to have the entire story read to them by this computer voice, or they could read the story themselves and simply get "help" on the words they didn't know. Each page of the "book" had a turned-down corner which one clicked to go to the next "page." On the picture page the pictures were clickable, with the computer voice speaking the identifying name of the picture when it was clicked. There was an option that presented the text of the book in alternative languages such as Spanish and Japanese.

The Broderbund Company has also produced software versions of popular children's books such as *Just Grandma and Me* by Mercer Mayer and *Arthur's Teacher Troubles* by Marc Brown. In these "living books" the child has the option of having the story read to her or exploring the story in an interactive fashion. When the story is read to the child each word in the book is highlighted as the computer voice reads it. In the interactive mode the child can click on a word and the computer voice will pronounce it. Animations and sounds are included in order to heighten the child's enjoyment of the story.

Teachers can use such software as a supplement to their classroom reading instruction. Although some teachers might object to the idea of a computer "reading" a "book" to a child, on humanistic grounds, there are some positive results that can come from this interaction. Obviously, in an ideal world all children will have the benefits of sitting on the lap of a loving adult while that adult reads children's books aloud. No computer can offer anything near a substitute for this most effective environment for shared reading. However, in reality some children are denied this experience. Their family situations are such that this kind of reading doesn't occur at home. At school there are simply too many children for each teacher: The individual attention that these children need is often unavailable. For such children the benefits of interacting with books through computers are worthwhile. While not a substitute for the human touch, this experience is beneficial to a child's reading. The child can "ask" the computer to read a word as often as is necessary. Through much repetition the child will begin to recognize words as sight words. The correct pronunciation of the word by the computer is assured. The child can read along with the computer voice as often as (s)he likes. The computer is infinitely patient.

Some of the books on CD offer additional features such as a choice of voice (male/female; adult/child), open-ended questions, and access to background information on the author and/or the book. These features add an important dimension to these products in that they encourage readers to take a more active role in interacting with the book. Whenever readers are encouraged or enabled to make choices about what they read, it encourages a reader-response, and this is an important element of constructivist learning. Such features of some of the books on CD will be appreciated by constructivist teachers.

One popular type of software for teaching reading in the last decade is software that presents decoding skills in the form of a game. A good example of software of this type is *Reader Rabbit* from The Learning Company. In this program children are presented with a variety of activities in which their attention is focused on beginning letters, middle letters, ending letters, word matches, and so on. In one activity a series of three-letter words moves onto the screen on an assembly-line conveyor belt. If the word has a matching letter to a target word, the child moves the word along on the conveyor belt. If a word does not match the target, the child drops that word into the trash. The target letters are the beginning letters in some exercises, the ending letters in some exercises, and the middle letters in other exercises. The format of the game is highly engaging for young children because it makes use of colorful, lively animation and catchy music. The children enjoy seeing Reader Rabbit dance when they get all of the words in a particular activity correct.

USING THE WORLD WIDE WEB

Teachers have reported that the Internet has tremendous potential as an aid in the teaching of language arts. Through e-mail, children can develop keypal relationships with children from all over the world, they can participate in listservs that are appropriate for children, and they can read and contribute to newsgroups. Using telnet or IRC* they can engage in live chat sessions in which they exchange views with other children in an environment moderated by adult leaders. Children's literature web-sites allow children to read and write reviews of their favorite books. Other sites center on popular authors of children's literature, and provide opportunities to correspond directly with some of those authors.

According to Mike (1996), the Internet can be used to promote such literacy skills as reading for a purpose, regulating reading rate, making evaluative judgments about text, and synthesizing textual information. Mike also notes that the World Wide Web allows students to publish information, which provides needed practice with both reading and writing. It promotes a sense of audience in both reading and writing (as in responding to newsgroups and listservs). It promotes literacy for an authentic purpose. It promotes communication within a social context, and social construction of meaning is enhanced.

Keypals

Keypal projects that are coordinated by classroom teachers abound on the web. Two sites that teachers use to locate appropriate keypals are KIDLINK† and Intercultural E-mail Classroom Connect (IECC). KIDLINK is devoted to promoting global dialog among children, and IECC's goals are similarly cross-cultural. At both of these sites the teacher can post a request for a specific type of classroom with which to correspond. A typical request may be as follows:

> A teacher of grade 2 (ages 7 and 8) in sunny Florida, USA, is seeking a keypal classroom for correspondence throughout this school year. We would like to connect with

---

*Internet Relay Chat: A system of hardware and software by which users engage in live discussions on-line. Participants type what they wish to say, and when they hit <enter>, their words are distributed to the screens of all participants. The name of the speaker is identified along with the speaker's words.

†Information about KIDLINK's keypal exchange is found at http://www.kidlink.org/KIDCAFE/help/keypals-a.html.

a classroom of children about our own age in an English-speaking country. We're especially hoping to find a keypal classroom that is outside the USA, and our preference is to connect with a non-tropical country. We'd like to begin by writing about cultural and climate differences. Please get in touch with me, Jonathan Flora, at jflora@schoolnet.net. Thanks!

This request has several features that make it easy for another teacher to respond. The teacher has identified both the grade level and ages of the children in the class. This is important because schools outside the United States use different grade-level numbering systems than do U.S. schools. The ages of the children are needed in order to communicate internationally. Secondly, the teacher provides a one-word description of Florida. Teachers from around the world may or may not know where Florida is or what its climate is like. Thirdly, the teacher is very specific about the type of classroom that he wants to correspond with. This is important because it allows potential partners to screen themselves before they respond. Finally the teacher identifies some of the things he plans to use the experience for: discussing cultural and climate differences. This allows teachers with similar goals to respond to the request. A vague request for keypals can easily lead to an unsuccessful experience if the two classrooms have widely different goals.

After this type of request is posted in the appropriate place on KIDLINK or IECC, or a similar organization's web-site, the teacher can expect to receive several replies. (It is important to find out where is the *appropriate* place to post such notices. It is considered bad netiquette to post requests for keypals in such places as listservs that are devoted to discussion of other topics, for example.) At that point the teacher might simply accept the first reply, or he may correspond once or twice with the respondents to try to find the one that would fit best. It is necessary for the teachers to correspond first in order to discover whether the e-mail programs that they are using are completely compatible. After the connection is established, the children write introductory letters. In most cases the children need to compose their letters off-line, using word processors.

As with any writing project, the teacher should provide clear guidance about what to write. After a cycle of editing and revising, each of the children should save their letters to a single document. Then the teacher can write an e-mail message to the teacher of the corresponding classroom and attach the document containing the student letters to the e-mail. (Most e-mail programs allow writers to "attach" a document or a folder to an e-mail message. This attachment is sent along with the e-mail. The recipient's e-mail program must have the capability to allow the recipient to open the attached file.)

An alternative way to find a keypal classroom, and in some respects a better way, is to look at a place like IECC to see the requests that are posted there by other teachers. If a suitable match can be obtained by answering someone else's request, it makes the system of posting requests more efficient.

Live Chats

Another component of KIDLINK is KIDLINK IRC, which is focused on bringing children together for live, on-line chats. Using telnet[1] or IRC client[2] software, a registered member of KIDLINK can participate in organized, scheduled chats on topics chosen by the leaders of KIDLINK IRC. Participation in such chats provides many educational benefits to children. Such benefits can include speaking (writing) to a live audience of international peers, listening to (reading) the contributions from a diverse group of peers, thinking about and responding to a wide variety of ideas about interesting topics, and formulating persuasive arguments. Since membership in KIDLINK IRC is required, there is some control over who participates in these chats. The organization is self-policing, so if any participant contributes in an inappropriate and harmful way they will be asked to leave the chat. Finally, there are adult moderators who participate in the chats in order to keep

---

[1] For on-line instructions for using telnet to participate in KIDLINK IRC, go to http://www. kidlink.org\IRC\telnet.html.

[2] IRC client software is more complicated to set up than is telnet, but use of it is easier after the initial setup. You can obtain instructions and help in getting IRC client software and getting it properly set up from the KIDLINK IRC web-site.

them focused on the stated topics. Teachers who want to participate in these organized chats can find a schedule and calendar at http://www.kidlink.org/english/calendar/calendar.html. Also, teachers can use the KIDLINK IRC listserv to post their own plans for chats at particular times and ask for participants to join them for a chat.

Children's Literature Sites

The web has an abundance of sites that are dedicated to promoting children's literature. A good place to begin exploring these is http://www.acs.ucalgary.ca/~dkbrown/index.html. At some of these sites children can find pages devoted to their favorite authors. In some cases the authors have made their e-mail addresses available to children who wish to write to them. At most of the children's literature sites, children can read reviews of their favorite books. Many sites provide children with the opportunity to write and publish their own review of a book. Furthermore, children can put their name and e-mail address on a list that notifies them when new books are published by their favorite authors, or when new books of a certain type or on a certain topic are published.

Creative teachers are folding these websites into their regular teaching of children's literature. Whereas in the past a child might have been required to write a book report that only the teacher would read, today children are being asked to write and publish on the web a review of that book for thousands of other children to read.

Other teachers use the web to build a community response to a piece of literature. *Daedalus Interchange** is a piece of software that allows students within a classroom to respond interactively to a piece of literature. With *Daedalus Interchange,* students can be given a literary prompt by the teacher and then they can each type their response to the prompt and then their responses to each other. A discussion might center around reactions to a chapter in a book

---

*From Daedalus Group, 1106 Clayton Lane, Suite #250-W, Austin, TX 78723. (808) 879-2144. http://www.daedalus.com/

that all the students had read. By encouraging reactions to the text and reactions to each other, a teacher using this method promotes a constructivist view of learning. The value of using this type of electronic communication in the classroom is questionable because face-to-face dialog would be preferable. However, similar products are being developed to allow such interaction to take place on the World Wide Web. In a circumstance where there is only one student in class who is interested in a certain book, this student will be able to enter into dialog with others like himself from around the world using Daedalus-like software and the World Wide Web.

DELTA PRINCIPLE PERSPECTIVE

Use of Tools

Since none of these tools was designed to help children learn language skills, all the uses that we've suggested represent either Delta Level II or Delta Level III uses. Using word processing for teaching writing, using databases for teaching information-locating skills, using visual organizers as an aid to writing, and using draw/paint tools represent Delta Level II. Using word processing interactively to help teach early reading would represent a Delta Level III use of the technology.

Prior to the introduction of technology that can turn spoken words into text on the screen, it was virtually impossible for a classroom teacher to give children *individual* experiences with this process. Teachers for many years have been turning the spoken words of a *class* into written text by creating "language-experience" charts. This has had great value in helping children associate spoken language with written language. However, the difference between a class experience and an individual experience is significant. In a class, the more vocal and "with-it" children are the ones whose words are often captured by the teacher and recorded on the language-experience chart. Even then, the teacher often has to paraphrase what the children have said in order to keep the number of words written to a reasonable number. Using the new technologies, the children who would ordinarily not contribute in a group setting can experience the delight of seeing *their* words recorded in print.

The children with a lot to say can experience the delight of seeing *all* their exact words recorded.

Additionally, the use of speech-to-text technology can re-define the way primary grade teachers use class time. Without the use of this technology teachers spend great amounts of class time creating the class language-experience charts. Using the technology, much of the creation of language experience stories can be done individually by children working one-on-one or in pairs at the computer. Additional class time is then made available for sharing of the stories created by the individual children. This increased sharing time is beneficial for building a sense of community within the classroom and for helping the children learn from one another.

Depending on the way in which the teacher uses it, word processing as an aid to teaching writing may well move toward a Delta Level III use of technology.

Use of Educational Software

Books on CDs would appear to be a somewhat weak application of computer technology. Why use a machine costing in excess of $2000 to present a story that is easily presented in a regular book? However, in the hands of a skillful teacher such software can provide helpful practice for beginning readers. Used in the interactive mode these books give the child the opportunity to explore unknown words and hear them pronounced repeatedly by the computer. A skillful teacher can encourage the beginning reader to work with the CD until (s)he feels confident to "read" the story aloud to the teacher or to the class. Such rehearsal for an authentic performance task can have a profound effect on the child's growing ability to decode and read expressively. Such a *use* of educational software would probably be classified as a Delta Level II use: It is moving in the direction of new uses of the technology, but it is not re-defining the way in which children learn to read. The availability of features such as choice of reader voice, open-ended questions, and access to background information on the author represent hints at some Delta Level III changes that may be in the future of books on CD.

The use of game software to practice decoding skills is also not using the technology at its highest level. Children enjoy the activities, and because of this they tend to get more practice with decoding skills than they might otherwise have, but such use does not *change the way in which children learn to read.* Since computers were not designed to provide decoding practice, we would classify this use of the computer as a Delta Level II use.

Use of the World Wide Web

As we've mentioned elsewhere in this text, use of the World Wide Web for K–12 education in general is a Delta Level II use of the technology. We are seeing more and more innovation from teachers concerning bringing this resource into the classroom in helpful ways. The use of Internet keypals has some advantages over an earlier generation's use of penpals. Because of the speed of electronic communication. a much larger volume of communication can take place than was possible with exchanges of letters. But, greater volume does not lead to a change in the nature of learning and teaching. The same can be said about children's literature sites on the web. The interactions that are facilitated by these sites were possible before the technologies existed. (Children have always been able to write to their favorite authors, for example.) The use of the web allows more immediate communication, but it does not dramatically alter the process of communication.

Audience is one area in which the World Wide Web has a distinct advantage over other technologies. In the past, much of children's writing was done for an imaginary audience or for the teacher only. Today, because schools are publishing on the web, children are writing for a legitimate audience. In many cases it is their peers from around the country and around the world who are reading their work. The impact of having children writing for a real audience could well lead to some Delta Level III changes in how children learn to write. One would expect that children will find it easy to be motivated to write well if they are writing for an audience. If our teachers can encourage children to be a constructively critical audience, the effects will be even greater. Imagine the effect on a 9-year-old writer if she receives feedback from a 7-year-old reader from across the country stating that her description of a character in her story was confusing.

Project-Based Learning

One way to begin to experience some Delta Level III benefits of technology for the teaching of language arts is to engage children in a publishing project that involves many different applications of technology. Penelope Dyer and Kathy Blond (1997) describe a web publishing project that exemplifies this approach to teaching. In their web publishing project the goal is to publish a web page related to a theme in the elementary curriculum. They begin by showing students examples of web pages that were developed with various purposes in mind (to inform, to persuade, to influence a purchase, etc.). The children examine these differing purposes for communication and answer questions such as, "What kind of information is this sharing?" "What is the purpose of this page?" "How does it communicate?" After leading the children in this examination, the teachers define the purpose of their project: They are going to design a multimedia report and present it on the web.

The next stage of the project is to use a visual organizer (like *Inspiration* or Claris Impact™) to brainstorm a concept map for the theme they will be studying. Following this, the children are asked to begin individual journaling to keep track of their developing knowledge about the thematic topic. (Dyer and Blond use *Student Writing Center* software from The Learning Company for this stage.) The children respond to specific prompting questions in their journals.

Later the students again meet together in a large group and the teachers (with student input) use a word processor to generate a list of questions that need to be explored. The children are to work individually or in small groups to do research to uncover answers to these questions. Their research includes electronic sources of information such as one of the encyclopedias on CD-ROM. Of course, the information that the students will find in such sources will be multimedia and not strictly text-based information. The teachers provide the students with simple forms to fill out to assist them with documenting their sources.

After a time of research (several days) the children are again called together as a large group to plan a storyboard for their web publication. A storyboard is a visual tool used to identify nodes of information and the links that are needed to tie that information together. Part of the function of a storyboard is to identify the medium (text, sound, video, etc.) in which the information will be presented. Another function of the storyboard is to assign responsibilities for portions of the project to individuals and groups. The storyboard serves as a masterplan for the development of the multimedia presentation. Since a storyboard is a visual tool, software such as *Inspiration* or Claris Impact™ is again put to use.

After the storyboard planning is completed, the students do the actual work of creating the multimedia presentation. The teachers conference with the small groups as this process unfolds to assist the children with actually producing creative work rather than simply cutting and pasting the work of others. Naturally, technology is used extensively at this stage: text is produced on word processors, illustrations are produced in draw/paint programs, appropriate photos may be scanned or located on the web (with proper citations of course).

Finally the children's work is brought together for publication on the web. Software such as Claris Home Page™ or *Web Workshop* is used to actually construct the web pages. These are examples of software that allow web authors to place text and graphic objects on the screen in the design and arrangement that they will be seen in published form on the web. Once the pages are created, the final step is publication. The teacher works with the web administrator for the school or the district to publish the pages and link them to the appropriate locations on the school's web page.

Such a project may seem out of reach to many readers. However, this is the sort of thing that today's forward-looking educators are doing with technology in the classroom. Today's children are developing multimedia authoring skills as well as electronic research skills in order to be fully prepared for the world that they will live in. The language arts skills that children are using today go far beyond merely reading, writing, listening, and speaking.

THINK ABOUT

- Respond to the following assertion: Today's children need less reading instruction than did former generations because more of the information received by today's children is in the form of graphic communication.

- Is it appropriate to include multimedia authoring skills within the language arts curriculum, as we've suggested, or should this be taught as a new curriculum area?

- Do the benefits of children's books on CD-ROM outweigh the disadvantages?

- If children can speak to their computers and see their words turned into text, will they have any motivation to learn to write?

- Do children still need to learn skills of using an index and using a card catalog? Can you identify any information-locating skills that are not needed by today's children?

- Is it appropriate to use school time to teach children to use draw/paint software to illustrate their stories? How will teachers and schools find the time to do so?

- Do the benefits of live chats on the Internet outweigh the disadvantages?

- What skills do teachers need to be able to teach today's language arts?

SELECTED REFERENCES

Anderson-Inman, L., and Knox-Quinn, C. (1996). "Spell-checking strategies for successful students." *Journal of Adolescent & Adult Literacy,* 39(6), 500–503.

Dyer, P., and Blond, K. (1997). "Using Internet resources and new media tools to develop language arts abilities." *National Educational Computing Conference,* Seattle, WA: NECC.

Guthrie, L., and Rosenzweig, L. (1997). "Integrating technology into primary grade language arts: Research on Apple's Early Learning Connections," *National Educational Computing Conference,* Seattle, WA: NECC.

Land, M., and Turner, S. (1996). *Tools for schools: Applications software for the classroom.* Wadsworth Publishing Co.

Mike, D. (1996). "Internet in the schools: A literacy perspective." *Journal of Adolescent and Adult Literacy,* 40(1), 4–13.

Swan, K., and Meskill, C. (1995). *Multimedia and response-based literature teaching and learning: A critical review of commercial applications* (Report No. 2.23). National Research Center on Literature Teaching and Learning; University at Albany; State University of New York.

10 Ethical Issues

LOOKING AHEAD

A few years ago one of the authors had the "opportunity" to act as a chaperone for a group of high school students' senior trip. During the 5 days that we were together one of the students, Gina, had a standard reply to any of my questions about the wisdom of a particular course of action. Gina's words: "What could possibly go wrong??". Gina opened her eyes wide and spoke with an exaggerated air of naivite, so both of us knew that she had a very good sense of what could possibly go wrong! However, her understanding of what could go wrong and my understanding were on somewhat different levels of development. My role was to help her see the deeper implications of some of her proposed activities.

In the same way, we understand that the reader comes to this point in the text with some understanding of the ethical implications related to computers and technology in the classroom. The purpose of this chapter is to challenge the reader to think more deeply than perhaps (s)he has thought up to now about these ethical issues. A theme that runs through the chapter is the theme of computer accessibility in the information age. As the computer has become the central tool in handling information, and as our economy has become more dependent on information, those with computer skills have become those who have access to economic advantages. Those without computer skills and knowledge are increasingly finding themselves left out of the economic mainstream. We will examine a number of issues that keep some segments of our society from gaining equitable access to the necessary computer knowledge and skills.

CAN YOU?

- Identify at least four areas where school budgets must support technology?

- Describe the difference between the reasons businesses and schools computerize and explain why those differences are important?

- Provide several points on which affluent and disadvantaged schools differ in terms of their use of technology?

- Differentiate between the computer literacy model and the curriculum integration model?

- Suggest some ideas for how the financial inequities between affluent and disadvantaged schools might be addressed?

- Describe differences between the way males and females react to computing technology?

- Describe differences between the way schools treat males and females in regard to technology?

- Offer some solutions for the gender inequities that exist concerning technology in schools?

- Describe several types of software licenses that schools have available to them?

- Outline some steps to take to maintain children's safety when their work is published on the Internet?

- Tell what the purpose of an Acceptable Use Policy is?

TEACHER LABORATORY

List as many reasons as you can think of why unequal access to computers by various subgroups within our population is problematic. Compare your list with lists generated by your classmates. After comparing lists, write a persuasive essay of 500 words or less aimed at a well-endowed foundation who might give a grant to a disadvantaged school.

Spend some time observing in a school's computer lab. Document any differences that you observe between girls' and boys' computer behavior.

RESOURCES AND EQUITY

The kinds of changes in teaching and learning that have been envisioned in this text will not come about without substantial investments in resources. The necessary resources fall into two broad categories: money and time. Financial resources are needed to purchase, maintain, and upgrade equipment and software. Money is needed to provide for teachers. Teachers need to be given release-time to develop their computer knowledge and skills and to maintain currency with a rapidly changing landscape. These allocations of resources must be ongoing rather than one-time investments.

To their credit, schools have been investing in computer technology for many years. When schools spend money on computers, however, there is a fundamental difference between their motivation and the motivation of other institutions. When a business finds that certain operations can be computerized, the decision of whether or not to invest in computerization is an economic one. If the money spent on computerization can be recovered in a reasonable amount of time by an economic savings brought about by computerization, the investment is made. In this case a decision *not* to computerize would be a decision that costs the company more money than the decision *to* computerize. Schools are in a very different situation. Money spent on computers in schools does not result in economic savings to offset the purchase. The reason to purchase computers in schools has not been for economic advantage, but rather, for the sake of what is right and necessary in preparing students for the future. In a business the final analysis has been, "We cannot afford to delay purchasing computers." In schools the final analysis has been, "Our children will need to learn about computers." A stark reality must be faced: The motivation for businesses to invest in computers is a stronger and more urgent motivation than is the motivation for schools to do so. Because of this, schools have often been criticized for being slow to computerize.

Even so, some schools have invested in computers. The idea of preparing our children to use computers has been compelling enough to allow affluent schools to find money for computer purchases. One of the major ethical issues we face today is the unequal investments in technology between our affluent and our disadvantaged schools. The issue of economic disparity is, of course, much larger than the focus of this text. Here we examine only the effects of this disparity on technology investments. The issue is this: Affluent schools are able to invest much more heavily in technology than are disadvantaged schools. Schools in regions of poverty tend to have older computers and less-trained faculty than do schools in regions of affluence. Entangled with the issue of economic disparity is the issue of differing visions for computer use between our affluent and our disadvantaged schools. Not only are our affluent schools better endowed financially, but they tend to be closer to the cutting edge concerning the role of computers in schools. In this text we have emphasized a vision in which computers and other technologies are used to improve the teaching and learning of all subject areas. We have developed a vision of computer use that is integrated into the curriculum. Our vision places the teacher's own use of computers in the forefront. This vision replaces an earlier and an inadequate vision in which children were taught *about* computers and taught to use computers in the way that businesses use them. In this older model, if computers were used in the regular curriculum they were most often used as drill-and-practice machines in an attempt to help children receive higher scores on standardized tests. (Branscum, 1992). In this older model the teacher was a neglected part of the picture: Teachers did not need to have and use computers themselves. We refer to this older model as a computer literacy model. Affluent schools tend to embrace the integration model while disadvantaged schools tend to embrace the computer literacy model (Piller, 1992).

One of the effects of this difference in vision is that as the integration model takes root in schools, teachers begin to notice the Delta Principle in operation. They become able to teach, and children become able to learn, in the new ways described in this text. These new ways of teaching and learning are dependent on technology. This provides a stronger mandate for providing up-to-date computer equipment than does the computer literacy model: Now computers are *needed* in order to teach the school subjects in the most effective way. Although it is still not the economic motivation enjoyed by businesses, it is a stronger motivation than is supplied by the "our children should know about computers" model. The result of these changes is that affluent schools become even more committed to developing their technology resources because they truly need these resources to support their programs. Meanwhile disadvantaged schools continue to provide curricula that are based on old technologies, but with an added course or program on computer literacy. The rich get richer and the poor fall further behind.

The road toward a solution to the financial inequities begins with an awareness of the problem. All those involved in education must realize that these inequities exist and that they exacerbate the gap between the "haves" and the "have-nots" in our society. Once this awareness exists, then is the time for vigorous, public debate about ways to solve the problem accompanied by positive actions to solve the problem. Disadvantaged schools that have overcome the obstacles have done so through a combination of measures including after-hour open labs, computers for loan, increased teacher-training, grants, local partnerships, using telecommunications to develop a sense of community, using mentors and role models, having high expectations for everyone, and nurturing internal leadership (Milone and Salpeter, 1996). A part of the solution for disadvantaged schools is public and private money that is available in the form of grants. Federal money is available to schools through avenues such as Eisenhower funds. Private companies such as AT&T have been generous in funding Internet connections for schools. In order to obtain grant money someone on the faculty or administration must be knowledgeable and skillful enough to write a winning grant proposal. These funds tend to be awarded on a competitive basis, and funding goes to the most promising programs. Fortunately, the affluent schools have no monopoly on grant-writing talent. However, it will take more than grant money to close the technology gap between affluent and disadvantaged schools.

A source of power that has not been tapped, and which might provide some leverage, is the collective bargaining power held by the teachers' unions. Although traditionally the major concern of these collective bargaining units has been issues related to terms of employment, it might be possible for enlightened teachers to use collective bargaining to insist on increased financial support for technology for the students. This suggestion might seem radical to those who have used collective bargaining for other ends, but it does have some potential that is worth pondering. Creative and new thinking will certainly be needed in order to solve the problem of disparate technology funding in our nation's schools.

The other resource, time, is not totally unrelated to finances. Money is needed in order to provide teachers with ongoing training regarding the use of technology in schools. In the early years of computers in education, the torch was carried by self-taught and self-motivated teachers who led the way. As we have moved to an awareness of the need for all teachers to integrate technology into the curriculum, there has been a corresponding increase in the need for faculty development and faculty training. If a school is to take advantage of technology, money must be continuously budgeted for technology training for the teachers. The situation here is not unlike the situation concerning purchase of computer equipment. Businesses cannot afford *not* to have their employees trained in the most cutting-edge skills, and so they invest in ongoing training for them. Schools, however, have expected teachers to gain computer skills on their own time, on their own initiative, and by self-instruction. This area of neglect has been costly to schools. The lack of teacher knowledge concerning the best potential of technology has been a major hindrance keeping schools from advancing into the benefits of Level III of the Delta Principle. Schools have only slowly come to realize that the teachers must be provided with release-time and structured, organized in-service training if they are going to be able to use technology to its fullest potential. A major part of increasing teachers' understanding of the benefits of computers is to provide them with computers for their professional use.

Time for training is not the only issue related to teachers' time. Even when the teachers have knowledge of the most powerful new technologies, it takes far more time to prepare lessons that make use of these technologies than it took to prepare lessons before. For example, in order for a teacher to do a credible job using a resource such as KIDLINK, she must spend hours each month keeping up with e-mail correspondence on a variety of listservs. Contacts must be made with people in various parts of the world, in all the different time zones. Ideas must be presented to others, discussed, modified, and published. All this activity takes a great deal of extra teacher time. The rewards are absolutely worth the effort, but it is unjust to expect teachers to add this to their already overburdened schedules.

Another example is the extra time required to prepare a computer-based presentation that makes selective use of video from an optical laserdisk. A typical optical laserdisk contains thousands of images. A teacher has to take the time to find the appropriate images and sections of video footage. Once the images are found, it takes time to assemble them into a form that can be used in a presentation. Then the presentation must be prepared. The resulting presentation is a far more effective teaching tool than any of the alternatives; it is worth the time spent in preparation. However, it is unjust to ask teachers to simply add this extra time to what they are already doing. Although technology can free some time for teachers when it is used to help manage the daily routine, technology becomes an added consumer of time when it is used to enhance lessons. At some point the extra time required for preparing technology-rich lessons must be taken into consideration in determining a teacher's workload. Without some adjustment to a teacher's workload in recognition of these extra demands, it is unlikely that very many teachers will invest the necessary time to prepare technology-rich lessons. Unfortunately the marketers of educational technology products have little motivation to inform educators about the time required to make good use of their products. Perhaps at some point teachers will demand products that are both easy to learn *and* educationally valuable.

GENDER

Questions about differences between the way boys learn and the way girls learn occupy a major component of educational research literature. In order to understand the ways that girls and boys relate to computers one must know a little about the general field of gender differences in education. Although boys' and girls' success in school, overall, is similar, how the genders perceive their level of success differs (D'Amico, Baron, and Sissons, 1995). When girls are successful, they tend to attribute their success to effort or luck. When they fail, they tend to attribute the failure to lack of ability. In contrast to this, when boys fail they tend to attribute their failure to bad luck. When boys are successful they attribute this to their abilities. The tendencies of girls to see their successes as due to luck and to blame themselves for their failures is known in the educational literature as "learned helplessness." Boys generally exhibit less learned helplessness than do girls.

This learned helplessness orientation is seen more in mathematics than it is in other school subjects. Traditionally computers and technology have been rooted in the mathematics/science domains. These domains have been generally perceived to be male domains. Therefore, the learned helplessness of girls is likely to affect their attitudes toward computers and technology to the extent that they perceive computers in the traditional way.

Much of the research into gender differences regarding computer use indicates that boys are benefitting more from computers than are girls. Some studies have shown that girls are less involved in computing than are boys (see Silvern, Williamson, and Countermine, 1988, for example.) There is some evidence, at least at the college level, that females are less comfortable than males regarding spreadsheets and databases (Sheffield, 1996). Some evidence indicates that girls may exhibit more anxiety and less confidence than do boys.

The research, in some ways, is inconclusive, however. Some researchers (Morse and Daiute, 1992) take issue with the fact that so much of the gender research has been conducted using inadequate research methods. According to these researchers, the most common research methods that are used to measure attitudes are themselves biased to produce results that overstate gender differences. Morse and Diaute conducted research in which they *observed* school children intensively as they worked with computers. In addition they asked *open-ended* interview questions of the children. (This is in contrast to asking children to respond to a series of strongly agree, agree, disagree, strongly disagree questions.) Using these research methods, they found no support for the conclusions of others that indicated higher anxiety, lack of interest in computers, or avoidance of computers among girls.

Although these findings do call into question some of the beliefs about gender differences related to computers, not all of the earlier research can be discarded on the basis of faulty methodology. Much dependable research, such as studies that have simply counted the number of females and males in elective computer courses, has indicated that girls are being benefitted by computers to a lesser degree than are boys. Although it is possible that the difference in attitudes toward computers is not as great as has been thought, there are still good reasons to believe that girls are using computers to a lesser degree than are boys. Teachers must be aware of these issues and guard themselves against contributing to the problem. Computers and technology are simply too important to the future success of our children. We must not permit there to be a disadvantage for 50 percent of our population.

One of the ways to mitigate gender differences might be to avoid forming mixed-gender groups for work on the computer. Since boys, on the whole, are more aggressive than are girls, a girl-boy pairing might be expected to be a disadvantage for the girl. The boy will be more likely to take control of the mouse and act as the decision-maker. D'Amico, et al. (1995) have observed some interesting differences between the ways boys and girls behave in groups for computer work. For boys an ideal group size seems to be two. For girls an ideal group size seems to be three or four. Teachers should try these different grouping arrangements on their own to see if their students respond like those in the research. Other resources for teachers who are interested in gender equity with regard to technology can be found at the following web site: http://gseweb.harvard.edu/TIEWeb/STUDENTS/STUDENTGROUPS/WIT/wit.html.

COPYRIGHT ISSUES

An ethical issue that is somewhat different from the ones discussed up to this point is the issue of copyright. The issue of copyright affects many areas of technology use. One area of concern relates to software licenses. Another area of concern is material found on the Internet. A third area of concern is the act of publishing materials on the Internet.

Software Licenses

Ownership of computer software is somewhat unusual. When a consumer purchases a book or other printed material, the consumer owns the book. When a consumer purchases computer software, the consumer owns a *license* to use the computer software. Typically a software license specifies the conditions under which the software may be used. Ordinarily the license permits the owner to make one copy of the software for archival (backup) purposes and to install one copy of the software on a computer's hard disk. The license specifies that only one computer may have the software installed. The license is found on an envelope that contains the disks on which the computer program is recorded. The license states that by opening the envelope the user is agreeing to abide by the terms of the license. (See Figure 10–1 for a sample of a software license.) Each school district will have a policy regarding the responsibilities of school personnel regarding software licenses. It is important for teachers to understand the issues behind these policies.

Illegal copying of a book would be a tedious and time-consuming operation. Illegal copying of a piece of computer software is extremely easy to do. It takes almost no technical knowledge, and no more than a couple of minutes of time to illegally copy a piece of software to one's hard disk. It is very common for otherwise ethical and moral people to ask for and/or offer illegal copies of software to one another. Since most commercial software has a selling price in the range of hundreds of dollars, there is great temptation for people to use illegal copying as a means of saving money. Teachers, especially, must be models of ethical behavior concerning this issue.

Commercial Software

Software manufacturers offer several different options for licensing software that will be used in schools. Ethical and legal behavior on the part of school personnel requires that school personnel know the type of license that the institution owns. In order of increasing cost, some common types of licenses and a few comments about them are shown in Table 10–1.

If a school owns a multiple-user license or some types of network licenses, it is the responsibility of school personnel to monitor the software to be sure that it is not being used by more than the maximum number of users as specified in the license. Some network licenses are programmed in such a way that the software itself monitors the number of simultaneous users and if extra users attempt to log on they receive a warning message and are not permitted access to the software until someone logs off. Some companies

LICENSING AGREEMENT

You should carefully read the following terms and conditions before opening this disk package. Opening this disk package indicates your acceptance of these terms and conditions. If you do not agree with them, you should promptly return the package unopened.

Allyn and Bacon provides this Program and License its use. You assume responsibility for the selection for the Program to achieve your intended results, and for the installation, use, and results obtained from the Program. This License extends only to use of the Program in the United States or countries in which the Program is marketed by duly authorized distributors.

License Grant

You hereby accept a nonexclusive, nontransferable, permanent License to install and use the Program on a single computer at any given time. You may copy the Program solely for backup or archival purposes in support of your use of the Program on the single computer. You may **not** modify, translate, disassemble, decompile, or reverse engineer the Program, in whole or in part.

Term

This License is effective until terminated. Allyn and Bacon reserves the right to terminate this License automatically if any provision of the License is violated. You may terminate the License at any time. To terminate this License, you must return the Program, including documentation, along with a written warranty stating that all copies of the Program in your possession have been returned or destroyed.

Limited Warranty

The Program is provided "As Is" without warranty of any kind, either express or implied, including, but **not** limited to, the implied warranties or merchantability and fitness for a particular purpose. The entire risk as to the quality and performance of the Program is with you. Should the Program prove defec-

tive, you (and **not** Allyn and Bacon or any authorized distributor) assume the entire cost of all necessary servicing, repair, or correction. No oral or written information or advice given by Allyn and Bacon, its dealers, distributors, or agents shall create a warranty or increase the scope of its warranty.

Some states do **not** allow the exclusion of implied warranty, so the above exclusion may **not** apply to you. This warranty gives you specific legal rights and you may also have other rights that vary from state to state.

Allyn and Bacon does **not** warrant that the functions contained in the Program will meet your requirements or that the operation of the Program will be uninterrupted or error free.

However, Allyn and Bacon warrants the disk(s) on which the Program is furnished to be free from defects in material and workmanship under normal use for a period of ninety (90) days from the date of delivery to you as evidenced by a copy of your receipt.

The Program should **not** be relied on as the sole basis to solve a problem whose incorrect solution could result in injury to a person or property. If the Program is employed in such a manner, it is at the user's own risk and Allyn and Bacon explicitly disclaims all liability for such misuse.

Limitation of Remedies

Allyn and Bacon's entire liability and your exclusive remedy shall be:

1. The replacement of any disk **not** meeting Allyn and Bacon's "Limited Warranty" and that is returned to Allyn and Bacon or

Figure 10–1.   A Sample Software License

2. If Allyn and Bacon is unable to deliver a replacement disk or cassette that is free of defects in materials or workmanship, you may terminate this Agreement by returning the Program.

In no event will Allyn and Bacon be liable to you for any damages, including any lost profits, lost savings, or other incidental or consequential damages arising out of the use or inability to use such Program even if Allyn and Bacon or an authorized distributor has been advised of the possibility of such damages of for any claim by any other party.

Some states do **not** allow the limitation or exclusion of liability for incidental or consequential damages, so the above limitation or exclusion may **not** apply to you.

General
You may **not** sublicense, assign, or transfer the License of the Program. Any attempt to sublicense, assign, or transfer any of the rights, duties, or obligations hereunder is void.

This Agreement will be governed by the laws of the State of Massachusetts.

Should you have any questions concerning this Agreement, or any questions concerning technical support, you may contact Allyn and Bacon by writing to:

Allyn and Bacon
Simon and Schuster Education Group
160 Gould Street
Needham Heights, MA 02194

You acknowledge that you have read this Agreement, understand it, and agree to be bound by its terms and conditions. You further agree that it is the complete and exclusive statement of the Agreement between us that supersedes any proposal or prior Agreement, oral or written, and any other communications between us relating to the subject matter of this Agreement.

Notice To Government End Users
The Program is provided with restricted rights. Use, duplication, or disclosure by the Government is subject to restrictions set forth in subdivision (b)(3)(iii) of The Rights in Technical Data and Computer Software Clause 252.227-7013.

Figure 10–1.   *Continued*

Table 10–1.   Common Types of Commercial Software Licenses

LICENSE TYPE	WHAT IS PERMITTED	SUITABILITY FOR SCHOOLS
Single-user License	Permits installation on one and only one computer.	Not usually economical for schools.
Multiple-user License (sometimes called a "Lab Pack")	Permits installation on up to a specified number of computers (typically 5, 10, 50, etc.).	Economical and commonly found in K–12 schools.
Network License	Permits installation on a network. License will specify the maximum number of simultaneous users.	Economical and commonly found in larger K–12 schools if they are networked.
Site License	Permits installation on any and all computers owned by the institution.	Not typically used in K–12 schools. More common for college campuses.

offer additional licenses to be added to a multiple-user license for minimal additional cost. Some companies allow teachers and students to install the software on their own computers at home if the appropriate number of licenses have been purchased. Unless this practice is specifically permitted by the type of license purchased, it is unethical and possibly illegal to do so.

You may be tempted to think that using a "pirated" piece of software causes no harm, but that is definitely not the case. One of the authors had spent several months of 22-hour days (yes, that is not a misprint!) creating a large instructional software package for a major publishing house. As a marketing gimmick, the publisher sent out thousands of copies of the software along with a letter instructing teachers to "buy it at our low price or simply return it after your review." As it turns out, nearly all the copies of the package were returned and very few were purchased. The publisher decided the software was not very good and took it off the market. The author then sent the package to the international leaders in reviews of instructional technologies for this particular field and was told that what he had written was excellent. In fact, they had singled his software out as one of a very small number of select programs that were highly recommended for purchase. This led him to believe that if it was that good, perhaps a few of the teachers who had returned the software may have retained an illegal copy. In any case, without the backing of the publishing company, the software never saw widespread use and now sits in boxes in his attic. His story is not unique. It turns out that many talented programmers recognize how difficult it is to recover the costs of developing good instructional software, let alone make a profit. This is exacerbated by the use of pirated materials. Of course, you also should consider the example you set for your students if they see you taking part in illegal activities. You don't allow plagarism of written materials by your students. Don't let them see you steal this newer type of "intellectual property."

Shareware

Not all software is developed and marketed by large, established software companies. Many programmers develop software on their own, and they are interested in marketing it themselves. Without the backing of a large company, they must find ways to make people aware of their software on their own. A common way of doing this is to offer the software as "shareware." Shareware is software that the user may obtain for a trial period free of charge. The software is sometimes made available on the Internet; other times it is included free of charge with the purchase of a computer; other times it may simply be passed along on floppy disks from user to user. After the trial period is over, the user is expected to either stop using the software or voluntarily send a small purchase price to the developer of the software. In some cases the payment of this fee is entirely on the honor system; if the fee is not paid, only the user's conscience will be affected. In some cases the shareware ceases to work after the initial trial period is over. The fee for shareware is almost always very minimal: $15 to $25 is common.

Teachers can contribute to the development of excellent software by examining and purchasing excellent shareware. Many times a successful shareware product will attract the interest of the larger software companies. If a large software company believes a product will be successful, they will invest in the product and take the responsibility for marketing it. This arrangement is much better for the author of the software than is self-marketing. It also results in the software being purchased and used by many more people than would be the case if it remained as shareware. If teachers use excellent shareware without paying the fee, it is unlikely that a major software company will realize the potential benefits of the shareware, and it is unlikely that they will invest in it.

Although these are the ethical reasons in favor of using shareware and paying the fee for excellent shareware, there are other reasons to avoid using shareware. Software that is offered as shareware is most often rather simple and unsophisticated software. It is rather rare that a highly useful and powerful educational application will be developed in this way. A teacher might have to examine many pieces of shareware before finding one that is of great use in the classroom. Most teachers lack the time to devote to this. Another reason to be cautious about shareware is the possibility that the shareware will be carrying a virus.

A virus is a set of computer instructions inserted into a program by a programmer with destructive intentions. The set of instructions is designed to cause damage to computer files, and it sometimes is designed to cause malfunctions to the computer. Viruses are written in such a way that they reproduce themselves whenever copies are made of the software in which they are found. Shareware is, unfortunately, a likely place to find computer viruses. In spite of the fact that authors of shareware take steps to ensure that their product is virus-free when they distribute it, people who create viruses find shareware to be an easy target. If a teacher is going to examine shareware, it is important to install virus protection software on the computer. Virus protection software detects viruses whenever a new file is copied to the computer. Most viruses can also be "repaired" by virus protection software.

Freeware

Another source of software is "freeware." As is implied by the name, freeware carries no obligation for payment to the software developer. Freeware is sometimes available on the Internet, sometimes it is offered in a package with the purchase of computer hardware, and sometimes it is simply distributed from user to user. There are a variety of reasons that a particular piece of software may be offered as freeware. The product may be subsidized by commercial backers who are using the software as a means of advertising. The product may be under development and the distribution of it is being used to help the developer find programming errors known as "bugs".* Or the software may be a beginning programmer's attempt to gain credibility. Because of the variety of reasons behind freeware there is also a variety of quality found in freeware. Some freeware, particularly that which is used as a means of advertising, may be excellent and very useful to teachers. Other freeware is not worth the time invested in examining it. As with shareware, freeware can be a source of viruses.

Freeware is only an ethical issue in the sense that some unscrupulous people may claim that software is freeware when it is not. In almost all cases, freeware is clearly labelled as freeware, either in the packaging or in a "Read Me" file that accompanies the software on its disk or in its downloaded file. If a piece of software lacks such labelling, it is wise to assume that there is a licensing cost to be paid in order to legally copy and use the software.

---

*Software distributed for this purpose is known as a "beta" version of the software. Users of "beta" versions of software can expect to find malfunctions in their software.

Material Found on the Internet

Software licenses are only a part of the concern about copyright. The Copyright Act of 1976 applies very broadly to creative works, whether they have been registered with the copyright office or not. The text of this law may be found on the web at http://www.law. cornell.edu/uscode/17/index.html. Copyright means that the original creator of the material has the exclusive right to reproduce and distribute copies of the work. If an author allows unrestricted copying, (s)he is, by this action, waiving the (copy)right. In the most stringent interpretation of the law, this applies to every creative product from books to internal memos. Obviously, the question to ask about copyright is not whether or not a piece of work is protected by copyright, but rather, is the author retaining the right to be the sole copier of the material. These questions become particularly important when the discussion centers on materials that are published on the Internet.

In a technical sense, when your computer displays a home page on the Internet, your computer is presenting a copy of the page that "exists" on a remote computer. Therefore, whenever you view something on the Internet, you are viewing a published copy of an original document. In some cases the producers of that original document make it clear that the material is copyrighted and may not be duplicated and used without permission from the copyright owner. Examples of this are syndicated cartoons that are published on the Internet. The syndicators of the cartoons make it very clear that any downloading and use of the cartoons without permission is disallowed. In other cases people publish materials on the Internet with no regard for whether or not the material is downloaded and re-used. If material is placed on the Internet with no restrictions, it is probably safe to assume that the author is waiving copyright privileges. A teacher wishing to make use of such materials is probably free to do so, if (s)he provides the proper credits and citations.

The other major issue for teachers regarding copyright is the issue of "fair use." According to copyright laws, there are certain circumstances under which copies of copyrighted materials may legally be made. Figure 10–2 provides the actual text of the copyright

§ 107. Limitations on exclusive rights: Fair use

Notwithstanding the provisions of sections 106 and 106A, the fair use of a copyrighted work, including such use by reproduction in copies or phonorecords or by any other means specified by that section, for purposes such as criticism, comment, news reporting, teaching (including multiple copies for classroom use), scholarship, or research, is not an infringement of copyright. In determining whether the use made of a work in any particular case is a fair use the factors to be considered shall include—

(1) the purpose and character of the use, including whether such use is of a commercial nature or is for nonprofit educational purposes;

(2) the nature of the copyrighted work;

(3) the amount and substantiality of the portion used in relation to the copyrighted work as a whole; and

(4) the effect of the use upon the potential market for or value of the copyrighted work. The fact that a work is unpublished shall not itself bar a finding of fair use if such finding is made upon consideration of all the above factors.

Figure 10–2.   Section 107 of The Copyright Act of 1976, Defining "Fair Use"

law as it defines "fair use." Fair use guidelines apply to material that is obtained from the Internet just as they apply to any copyrighted materials. If a teacher is interested in using materials from the Internet, (s)he must be sure to do so within the constraints of this provision of the law. If the use of such materials will exceed fair use, it is necessary to write and obtain permission from the owner of the copyright.

It is important to note that it is not just textual material that is protected by copyright. On the World Wide Web there are graphic materials, audio materials, and video materials in addition to textual materials. Any of these various media may at some time prove helpful in teaching. Any of these media can be easily downloaded and used in teacher-made presentations.* Before such materials are freely used, the teacher must consider copyright laws and restrictions. At the very least, proper credit must be given for the source of all materials obtained and used.

---

*Downloading is accomplished from within a browser program by clicking and holding on a link and following the pop-up directions that appear.

Publishing Material on the Internet

Teachers and classrooms all over the world have entered a new level of use of technology by developing and publishing their own sites on the World Wide Web. When teachers assemble materials for their class web-sites, they must keep in mind that everything that is presented is essentially being published worldwide. Any materials that were not created by the students or by the teacher must be clear of copyright infringement. Teacher-made and student-made materials are protected by copyright, and if the authors of those materials do not want them freely distributed they must so state.

Aside from copyright concerns there are other concerns related to publishing children's work on the Internet. Children must be protected from anyone who might want to use the Internet to bring them harm. There should never be enough material of a personal nature published to enable someone to identify the children in the class. Photos of children should only be published if there is no other identifying information. First names are permitted with children's work if there is no photo. Since the school and community can be readily identified from the web page, it is never a good idea to publish children's last names. If there are ever any doubts about how much information to make available, it is wise to choose the most conservative and safest course: Publish less information rather than more.

THE UNSAVORY SIDE OF THE INTERNET

Much publicity has already been centered on the unsavory side of the Internet, but we would be irresponsible if we completely ignored it here. Even though only a tiny percentage of the people using the Internet have harmful ends in mind, they have received more than their share of attention. Consider the Internet to be like a city made up of the 20 million or so worldwide users. As with any city, there is a small portion of the population that is corrupt. Wherever large gatherings of people exist, the small percentage of the population that desires to harm people becomes enough of a force to attract attention. Even if a mere *one one-hundredth of one percent* of the worldwide Internet users had harmful intent, that would amount to 2,000 people. (This statistic is for illustration only. No estimate is being made of the actual number of problematic Internet users.) Two thousand people with evil intent are enough to attract attention, but they represent only the tiniest fraction of Internet users. In this illustration they would be outnumbered 1000 to 1 by the 19,998,000 virtuous users. This numerical comparison is only important to illustrate the vast quantity of beneficial resources that exist on the Internet. Schools that decide to keep the Internet out of reach of children because of the potential for harm are doing their students a great disservice.

Having put the harmful Internet users in their numerical place, we must discuss some of the options teachers and parents have for protecting children from these corrupt users. Certainly the most important influence on children is the home. Children who come from homes where pornography is not permitted, where sexual deviance is not tolerated, where abuse of children is unheard of, and so on, will have little appetite for these things when they explore the Internet. Since schools cannot control the home environments, they must be realistic, and they must realize that some children will seek out pornography on the Internet. Because of this, schools have taken a two-pronged approach to dealing with this problem. They have installed software that filters the sites that schoolchildren can access on the Internet, and they have developed Acceptable Use Policies (AUPs) to govern how schoolchildren are permitted to use the Internet. The filtering software is designed to disallow access to specific sites and to sites that use specified keywords. The difficulty with software of this sort is that the Internet is an ever-changing landscape. In order for any software of this sort to be fully effective, someone must monitor the Internet to discover the newly developed unacceptable sites and include them in the list of sites disallowed by the software. This is an undesirable task, to say the least.

Acceptable Use Policies are generally written in the form of agreements that schoolchildren or their parents must sign before they are given the opportunity to use the Internet. The benefits of such an agreement are twofold: First, they communicate to schoolchildren and their parents the kinds of behaviors that are expected and those that will not be tolerated. Second, they give the school the ability to remove a student's Internet privileges if the AUP is violated. While these benefits do not guarantee that no student will abuse his or her Internet privileges, they provide a reasonable level of control.

Aside from these controls probably the best measures that schools can take to guard against unacceptable use of the Internet are the positive measures. Schools that are actively involved in on-line curriculum projects will have their computers in use most of the time for structured, positive, global curriculum experiences. Teachers who take an active role in the use of the Internet for their teaching will know who is doing what on the Internet. Keeping the students productively busy most of the time goes a long way toward prevention of the undesirable uses of the Internet.

SECURITY

Unauthorized access to computers can pose many problems. In schools, the most sensitive materials are students' academic records and employee's personnel records. Some or all of this material is likely to be stored on computers. The risk of someone gaining unauthorized access to a stand-alone computer is rather small in comparison to the risk of someone gaining access to a networked computer. The risk of someone tampering with computers in an elementary school is lower than the risk of someone tampering with computers in a high school. Regardless of the comparative level of risk, any teacher who is storing sensitive materials on a computer must be aware of the possibility of unauthorized access and must take steps to prevent it.

The minimum of protection can be obtained by using software that provides password protection. Such software is installed as part of the operating system of the computer and it operates in the background. There are several types available. One type is activated when the computer is turned on: The startup of the computer is stopped until the appropriate password is entered. A second type operates when the computer is already on but has been inactive for a specified period of time. A move of the mouse, or a press of a key brings a request for a password. No activity is permitted until the correct password is entered. These two types of password protection should be used together.

A person seriously seeking to gain unauthorized access to a computer would use computer software to determine the password. In order to make it difficult for someone to figure out what your password is, you should choose a password that is not a word in a dictionary, has at least 8 characters, and has at least one non-alphanumeric character. (Characters such as # $ % are non-alphanumeric.) Even with the proper protections it is not impossible for a serious "hacker" to gain unauthorized access.

The increasing use of technology in schools opens many levels of concern for ethical issues. One of the major goals of education has always been to reinforce the prevailing values of the society. Today this includes helping children and young people learn to apply those values to the increasingly complex world of technology.

THINK ABOUT

- Why should Americans that live in affluent areas be concerned about inequities in terms of funding for technology in disadvantaged schools?

- Why might teachers' associations (teachers' unions) be reluctant to pressure school boards for more financial support for technology?

- Why are grants an inadequate solution for funding inequities?

- People sometimes criticize teachers for being slow to adapt their teaching to the technologies that are available. Is this criticism justified?

- Are there biological reasons that girls and boys differ in their reactions to computers? Why do you feel this way?

- Do you have any bias in terms of your expectations of boys versus girls and their use of computers? How do you know?

- What harm can it cause if people make unauthorized (illegal) copies of software? Try to identify long-range and indirect implications.

- Describe a hypothetical situation in which a teacher would be permitted to make copies of something found on the Internet under the auspices of "fair use."

- A school board has decided not to connect their school to the Internet because of the potential that students will access pornography. Develop a speech to use to try to persuade this school board to change its mind.

SELECTED REFERENCES

Branscum, D. (1992). "Educators need support to make computing meaningful." *Macworld* (September), 83–88.

D'Amico, M., Baron, L. J., and Sissons, M. E. (1995). "Gender differences in attributions about microcomputer learning in elementary school." *Sex Roles, 33*(5/6), 353–385.

Milone, M. N., and Salpeter, J. (1996). "Technology and equity issues." *Technology and Learning, 16*(4), 38–47.

Morse, F. K., and Daiute, C. (1992). *I LIKE computers versus I LIKERT computers: Rethinking methods for assessing the gender gap in computing* (No. ED 349 939).

Piller, C. (1992). "Separate realities." *Macworld* (September), 218–231.

Sheffield, C. J. (1996). "An examination of self-reported computer literacy skills of preservice teachers." *Action in Teacher Education, 17*(4), 45–52.

Silvern, S. B., Williamson, P. A., and Countermine, T. M. (1988). "Young children's interactions with a microcomputer." *Early Childhood Development and Care, 32,* 23–35.

Glossary

absolute reference: in a spreadsheet, a reference to a cell that does not change in relation to the changes in the cells that refer to it.

asynchronous: occurring at different points in time.

behaviorism: a philosophical orientation that centers on the outward behaviors of learners.

beta: a *beta* version of software is a version that has been released to end users, but which is still being tested for errors.

binary: using a base-2 number system.

browser: a piece of software that allows exploration of the World Wide Web.

chat-room: a metaphorical meeting place. Users communicate by typing. Everyone currently on-line on the same channel sees what is typed along with an identifier to designate who did the typing. Participants respond to one another by typing back and forth. Since any participant can be typing at any time, messages and thoughts are sometimes difficult to follow. It is not unusual for a comment and a reply to be interrupted by several messages on a different topic entered by different participants.

constructivism: a philosophical orientation that focuses on the mental constructs or schemas of learners.

digitize: to put into a format that is readable by computers.

download: to make a copy of a computer file or program from a distant computer to your own local computer.

hyperlink: a non-sequential connection between two distinct pieces of information or data on computers.

hypermedia: a system of linked pieces of information or multi-media files.

hypertext: a system of linked pieces of textual information.

Integrated Learning System   (ILS): a piece of software that presents learning tasks, keeps track of student performance on those tasks, and makes performance information available to the teacher.

Internet Relay Chat   (IRC): a live, on-line, typed discussion carried on between and among participants that are separated by distance.

links: connections between pieces of information or data.

listserv: an e-mail mailing list that distributes mail to all participants on the list and to which any participant can publish mail.

multimedia: having more than one of the following media: text, graphics, sound, video.

navigation: following hyperlinks in a hypermedia or hypertext environment.

nodes: locations in a hypermedia or hypertext environment; distinct units of information.

operating system   (OS): the computer programming code that instructs the computer how to operate. The operating system determines the type of human-computer interface.

relative reference: in a spreadsheet, a reference to a cell that is in relation to the cells that refer to it.

simulation: a computer game or environment that simulates some aspects of reality.

systemic: having to do with an entire system.

technophobe: one who has an inordinate fear of technology.

upload: to copy a computer file from a user's computer to a server.

virtual: an experience or a place that only exists in a technology-induced imagination.

Index